Creative Intelligences

Creative Intelligences

Edited by

Richard Gregory and Pauline K. Marstrand

for Section X of The British Association
for the Advancement of Science

 Frances Pinter (Publishers), London

© British Association for the Advancement of Science, 1987

First published in Great Britain in 1987 by
Frances Pinter (Publishers) Limited
25 Floral Street, London WC2E 9DS

British Library Cataloguing in Publication Data

Creative intelligences.
  1. Intellect   2. Artificial intelligence
I. Gregory, R. L.   II. Marstrand, Pauline K.
153.9   BF431

ISBN 0-86187-673-3

Typeset by Spire Print Services Ltd, Salisbury, Wiltshire
Printed by Biddles of Guildford Ltd.

Contents

Introduction

Professor Richard L. Gregory

Each year, the venerable, though in spirit youthful, British Association for the Advancement of Science meets in a different University City of the Kingdom of the British Isles. The venue for 1986 was Bristol. Bristol was at its peak in the eighteenth century: when its port was the second largest in the Kingdom, and it was the centre for the merchants of tobacco, wine (especially sherry) and, in its recent history, of dubious dealing in slaves. In fact, it must be confessed, its fortunes are largely based upon the selling of sin. As is so often the case, however, this produced some excellent architecture and a general spirit of well-being.

The British Association draws together about 3,000 people each year—youngsters, teachers and scientists—from all over the country, and indeed from abroad to talk, to meet each other, and in present circumstances to deplore the inadequate funding of their lives' work —which, at least as they see it, is aimed at making the present supportable and a viable basis for the future through inculcating learning, teaching, and research. It is indeed difficult to imagine more worthy activity. But then if Bristol's past (of which it is of course, seriously, justly proud) is anything to go by, sin seems to do better than intelligence.

The BAAS is organized into several sections, each with its own special Letter (such as 'J' for psychology) and each—under its general President—with its own Officers, who wear bejewelled medallions. The sections are organised by the Recorders (who have a medallion, for public recognition) and the Secretary (who does not). The Recorder was one of the editors: Pauline Marstrand. The Secretary was Dr. John Durant.

Apart from the serious side of a concentration of lectures and discussions on all manner of scientific issues and social implications, with the occasional excitement of a new discovery, the Annual Meeting traditionally has several highly enjoyable social events. These include a city reception, in which we were honoured by the

Lord Mayor. Each section has its dinner. Our's (Section 'X') was shared with Section 'J's, and was held in the delightful mansion, Goldney Hall, owned by the University. The Dinner, organised by Dr. John Harris and John Barrett—which was in the Orangery, surrounded by gardens including a formal lake, a magic grotto and a folly tower—was gilded by the generosity of the publisher Mr. Adam Gelbtuch (who owns the journal *Perception*) and by the generous contribution of the Institute for Scientific Information. These generosities greatly enhanced the culinary and also the libidinous (in the sense of 'libation' rather than 'libido') quality of the occasion, while placing it within the restricted pocket of the 'X' and 'J' academics and students. Normally science aims at truth through observation; but this party was graced with the remarkable conjuring abilities of Simon Watkins who succeeded in separating appearance from reality with dramatic effect.

The chapters in this book represent the papers presented at Section 'X'. Section 'X' is special—it is the 'General' section, which can deal with any topic. The topic is chosen partly by the Section Committee (which puts in a lot of work each year) and by the President for the year. I had the honour of being President for 1986, when the subject was the very general topic: 'Intelligences'. And of course I sported my Medallion, though with a hope that I would not be confronted too much in public by superior intelligences. Whether this happened or not, the entire occasion was intellectually stimulating for all of us and immense fun.

During this week the EXPLORATORY Hands-On Science Centre held an exhibition, in the centre of the city in the docks at Watershed. This was opened by the President of the British Association—who was about to become President of the Royal Society—Sir George Porter, PRS. It is pleasant to be able to report that, following this auspicious start, a few months later the EXPLORATORY opened on a daily basis to the public in the neo-Classical building, the Victoria Rooms, near the University in Clifton. The EXPLORATORY is designed to enhance the human intelligence of both children and adults, by hands-on interactive experience with working demonstrations and experiments. These are called 'Plores' for exploring, and they do indeed attract people of all ages and induce the delight of discovery.

The chapters of this book represent life-long cogitations of authorities in the broad field of intelligence. The topics range over the development of intelligence in the evolution of species, and its development in children, to intelligent machines, creativity, and puzzling questions of how far intelligence is based on knowledge and knowledge based on intelligence.

Richard L. Gregory
The University of Bristol

1 Intelligence based on knowledge — knowledge based on intelligence

*Richard Gregory**

There is a paradox in how we think of intelligence. We say that someone who does well by using special knowledge must be intelligent; but we also say that intelligence is demonstrated by succeeding without special knowledge. Thus, we assign intelligence both for lack and for presence of knowledge.

What, then, is intelligence? In normal English the word 'intelligence' has two meanings. Its earlier, and now less used, meaning is essentially *knowledge*, especially hot news, or gossip, or secrets of war. We find this use in 'military intelligence', which does not mean that the military are particularly bright; but only that they have, or seek, special information. Shakespeare's use of the word, in *Macbeth*, is in this sense: 'Say from whence you owe this strange intelligence?' This is the way the word is used before modern psychology.

The new, technical sense refers to IQ (intelligence quotient) tests, designed especially for comparing abilities of children. Such tests were first designed by the French psychologist Alfred Binet (1857–1911), in collaboration with Théodore Simon. Binet was asked at the beginning of this century by his government to find a way of distinguishing between children who were too lazy to learn and children incapable of learning through lack of ability. The aim was to save educational resources for the children who would benefit. But neither these nor later intelligence tests tell us what intelligence is, or what makes man so special compared with other animals. Perhaps, however, this is not a criticism, for much the same is true of measurements in even the most highly respected physical sciences. Thus, a thermometer is useful though it does not tell us what heat is, or what physically underlies the scale of temperature. On the other hand, temperature measures were necessary for discovering that heat is merely molecular agitation rather than a special substance (Caloric).

*Professor of Neuropsychology and Head of Brain and Perception Laboratory, University of Bristol

Temperature is measured along a single dimension (though with alternative conventional scales) as there is only one kind of heat—molecular agitation of greater or lesser degree. But it is far from clear that intelligence is at all like this. Is there really only *one* kind of intelligence—so that we can all be measured, and judged and compared, on the same (IQ) scale? We readily accept that the temperature of anything may be measured on a single scale (though different kinds of thermometers are necessary) for the human body, eggs, molten steel and stars; but, as Sir Peter Medawar (1977) has cogently argued it is far from clear that there is a single dimension of intelligence, to justify arranging us on a line from dim to bright.

Binet and Simon set problems which were graded along a single dimension in difficulty. By finding out which could be carried out by 50 per cent of the sample of children, in each age group, they established standardised performance scores for each age. Binet defined intelligence so that each individual child's IQ remains essentially constant as he or she grows up—though of course abilities improve enormously from infancy up to adolescence. In spite of the increase in abilities the average IQ score for children of all ages was set at 100 points; which was done by adjusting performance scores, by handicapping for age, up to the age of sixteen. Thus IQ is defined as mental age × 100/chronological age. It is important to note that abilities of children of different ages are not given directly from IQ scores—as abilities improve with increasing age though the IQ scores remain (on average) unchanged.

So IQ scores are not straightforward measures of ability; for they are 'corrected' for normal expected development of skills with age by the mental age/chronological age quotient. The measured ability/age quotient notion breaks down for adults, as there is no improvement for the kinds of ability that are tested for IQ after adolescence—although we go on getting older, and sometimes wiser! So if one had a measured IQ of 100 points as a child, it would sink to 20 points at the age of fifty, if the quotient procedure were extended into adulthood. If all children developed at the same rate, and in the same way, each child's IQ would of course remain constant; but there are different development rates, and the early tests are not always reliable predictors. There are frequently considerable changes of IQ scores through childhood, so even if one does accept IQ scores at face value, as tests of basic intelligence, there can still be optimism that a poor early score will improve. If a child is branded as having a low intelligence, or is hailed as a genius with an IQ of, say, 140+, his parents and teachers are apt to see him in this light. He is expected to remain dull, or to flower into genius, and these expectations can have marked effects. This is shown in experiments in which children are introduced into schools with made-up exceptionally high IQ scores: this boosts them to do rather better than children with the same scores. This is so also for animals in laboratory learning experiments; if the handlers believe some animals to be special, they tend to become special, which is a major reason for 'double blind' experiments.

In order to measure intelligence, however conceived, it is necessary to test observable abilities or skills. But intelligence is not simply performance or ability. It is supposed to underly abilities, from the simplest problem solving to the works of genius. But unless it is thought of as some kind of special (Caloric-like) substance that we possess, in more or less degree, to understand intelligence we need to know the brain's processes and internal procedures by which we solve problems and invent. This kind of understanding is, however, the aim of cognitive psychologists rather than, at least until recently, designers of IQ tests, who are more concerned with comparing individuals than with understanding what it is to be intelligent. It may, however, be practically impossible to compare intelligences without a theoretical understanding of how intelligence works, which is one reason why computer-based artificial intelligence is important in human terms.

Let us return, though, to the two meanings of 'intelligence': possessing knowledge that is *given*, and ability to *discover* and build knowledge. I suspect that thinking about intelligence has been strangled through not disentangling these what-is-given from what-needs-to-be-discovered senses of intelligence.

If the solution to a problem is already known there is no problem to solve. So, problem-solving ability (which is, essentially, what psychologists take as 'intelligence') must be assessed in the *absence* of sufficient knowledge. And if knowledge is required to solve the problem it is important, to be fair, that all the candidates start with the same relevant knowledge. When special knowledge is required comparisons between individuals' 'intelligence' is extremely difficult. Thus, we should expect the musician and the politician to have different kinds of knowledge and so to do very differently on many tests, even though they are equally 'intelligent'. The question is: if they have different knowledge bases, how can we compare their intelligences? This is a problem for comparing children and a much greater problem for adults, who have very different experiences.

One way of isolating the problem-solving of intelligence is to devise tests which do not require special knowledge; or to devise tests requiring only knowledge almost anyone may be expected to have. Another way is to accept that different knowledge-bases will affect performance—but somehow *handicap* people according to their special knowledge. This means, for example, that a history student would get fewer marks for questions on Rome, or the Middle Ages, than a physics student would earn though he comes up with the same answers. So if asked: 'What date was the Magna Carta?' And also: 'What is the gravitational constant?' they would be marked differently for identical answers. The difficulty here, with this second method, is to know how to apply fair handicaps for special knowledge. The problem over the first method (avoiding special knowledge altogether) is twofold. First, one cannot be sure that special knowledge is not involved; secondly, tasks not requiring special knowledge may seem trivial, even insulting, and so may not be performed well. It may, indeed, be that deploying one's knowledge is the most important feature of intelligence. To test people apart from what they have taken the trouble to learn and what they feel secure in may be to miss just what the tester should be looking for: ability do make effective use of knowledge. Some recent intelligence tests do stress the importance of drawing effective analogies, which must come from available knowledge. These tests may be on better lines and better reflect the knowledge-based nature of intelligence.

The problem of how much knowledge is involved in solving intelligence-test problems is especially important for claims that different races or the sexes have, on average, different intelligences. It is quite obvious that people with different racial backgrounds tend to have different experiences, and the same applies to the sexes. So how can races, or the sexes, be fairly compared? One approach is to try to devise tests free of special knowledge; but for comparisons between races this is extremely difficult, perhaps strictly impossible. To take an extreme example; for people with some cultural backgrounds, even the situation of being tested, of having to sit down and concentrate on working out problems and answering questions, is outside their experience. If the second strategy is adopted—to apply 'handicaps'—it is hardly possible to handicap fairly, because it is virtually impossible to assess the effects of cultural differences apart from performance at skills—which makes the situation logically circular.

Let us grasp the nettle and consider, in these terms, claims that men are more intelligent than women. Or, if you prefer, that women are more intelligent than men. In either case, a score suggesting one of these possibilities might be due to the testers having chosen questions or test tasks which are more familiar to the one sex than the other. The greater familiarity, or knowledge, will produce a higher score—but will this indicate greater intelligence? It could signify a lower intelligence. To justify this we would have to know the contribution made by the knowledge, which it is extremely difficult to do. And if there is a genetic component here, it may lie outside what is taken as intelligence. For example, it might lie in physical strength (for tasks such as changing wheels on cars) which makes the task easier, so it requires less intelligence. Even if the test does not involve physical strength, which is clearly sex-related, it may involve experience which has been more easily gained by physically stronger people. Similarly, one can think of converse examples favouring women, for example by their greater dexterity.

However all this may be, there is no doubt that if one asked a sample of men and women the following questions, men would generally do better than women in our society: what does the differential gear in a car do? What is a tee? What does a halyard have to do with blocks and cleats? What is the difference between stocks and shares? But a better score for these questions would be no particular indication of greater intelligence in the sense of more powerful problem-solving ability. For it happens that men in our culture tend to be more interested than women in golf, sailing and investments, as well as in mechanical principles—though of course there are plenty of exceptions. Similarly, if men and women were asked 'What a roux is, what fennel is used for, or what a pommel is', then women might be expected to do better. This means that a test which included a lot of the first items would favour men, while the kinds of items of the second test would favour women. So the result will largely depend on whether the tests are men-favouring or women-favouring. There are physiological differences between the sexes which make some tasks slightly easier for men or for women.

If tests come out with the answer that men and women have *equal* intelligence, this could be due to a successful balancing act by the test designers—to give equal men-favouring and women-favouring test questions. Then the claim that men and women have equal intelligence means merely that the test designers have got their balancing act right to bring about this result. If, on the other hand, they claim that men are more intelligent or that women are more intelligent, this could mean that they have presented too many men-favouring, or too many women-favouring questions—they have got their balancing act wrong. In neither case do we learn about relative intelligences; unless indeed it was shown that measured differences are too great for such an explanation.

This is only the beginning of a complicated situation which has a forest of logical and statistical traps. There is, also, the academic prejudice that academic abilities should be rated highly in the intelligence stakes; so a successful physicist will generally be rated 'higher' than a successful farmer or mechanic. But this may be little more than a reflection of academic arrogance; and of course it is academic psychologists who design intelligence tests.

Can we think more clearly about intelligence? We started by pointing out that the word 'intelligence' has two meanings, the older being given knowledge, and the second, ability to discover or build knowledge. In this second problem-solving, 'psychologists'' sense, knowledge is also important, but in a somewhat paradoxical way. For as we have more knowledge so problems are more easily solved. So, as we possess more of the first sense of intelligence,—we need less of the second sense. Until, with sufficient knowledge, the problem may disappear until we need no problem-solving intelligence. This is a paradox suggesting that it is appropriate to ascribe more intelligence to those who have less knowledge, though we generally associate having a lot of knowledge with high intelligence. This is a muddle that needs sorting out.

The first step, I think, is to recognise that knowledge in any form is always *produced* by some kind of problem-solving. So attaining knowledge requires problem-solving intelligence. Secondly, we may think of knowledge as 'frozen' problem-solving. Knowledge expressed in words, equations—or useful tools or technology—may be selected and 'thawed' for more-or-less immediate use. Thus, once scissors are invented, they solve the problem of cutting paper or cloth. This notion is very like the physical concept of *kinetic energy*, building up *potential energy* which may be used in various ways, such as by pumping water up to a reservoir, for producing electricity for any number of uses. So, using 'knowledge' very broadly, we may suggest the terms *kinetic intelligence* for knowledge production, and *potential intelligence* for the power of knowledge to solve problems. These are the two senses of 'intelligence' that we started with.

On this account, potential intelligence is *available* solutions and answers—which were *created* (perhaps in the distant past) by kinetic intelligence. If our present knowledge is adequate for a current problem or task, then little or no problem-solving—and so little or no kinetic intelligence—is required. Similarly for tools; if we have the right tools a job is much easier than if we have to invent a new tool or process. In this sense tools, as well as books and computer programs, are potential intelligence though they are not in brains. Kinetic intelligence is needed whenever a situation is somewhat novel; for then it is necessary to see how the available tools or symbolically stored knowledge may be applied—which requires an inventive leap or kinetic intelligence.

The issues here are bound up with novelty and creativity. It is absurd to consider intelligence separately from creativity, though test designers have minimised originality as it is so hard to measure. And much as small kinetic energy may release vast potential energy, a small creative step may produce dramatic consequences, for good or ill. So, as potential intelligence builds up over generations the world becomes both more promising and more dangerous. This suggests that although our kinetic intelligence is now less important in many situations, as we have more knowledge than our ancestors, yet it is more important in unfamiliar situations as the range of possibilities, including disasters, is greater.

However this may be, I think we can now see, in these terms, some essential difficulties in the business of measuring intelligence. The major difficulty is that the contribution of stored potential intelligence is overwhelmingly greater than that of the small inventive steps of kinetic intelligence. So the kinetic intelligence that psychologists try to measure is in most situations swamped by the power of knowledge. It is not clear that the kinetic intelligence of problem-solving can be isolated, for measurement, from the immense contribution of the stored knowledge of potential intelligence. We might define intelligence as *the generation of successful novelty*; but this is extremely hard to measure as the novel component of skills is so small.

It is not only living organisms that generate the successful novelty we see as intelligence. Novel solutions are generated most dramatically by the unintentional processes of organic evolution. It is, indeed, striking that the randomness and selection-by-success of evolution has solved inumerable problems (such as photosynthesis) which are beyond individual invention or understanding and remain unsolved by science. Even the simplest living organisms are supreme examples of potential intelligence, as they are solutions to incredibly difficult problems, which were solved over millions of years by the brainless blind steps of natural selection. So although plants are hardly intelligent in the kinetic intelligence sense of the psychologists, they embody immense potential intelligence as created through evolution, though its processes are blind.

And now: what of computers, that are beginning to be intelligent, as they build generalisations and apply analogies from their pasts to solve problems? Will they be blind intelligences, like the organic evolution that is our origin? Or will they, like us, have some understanding, goals, and directed intention to solving problems? If so, will their intentions match ours? Or will intelligent computers lift us out of our biological origins, into a new world of silicon—where our heritage of potential intelligence no longer applies? Then, intelligences that we have created may destroy us by their alien knowledge.

References

R. L. Gregory (1981), *Mind in Science*, London: Weidenfeld and Nicolson.
Sir Peter Medawar, (1977), 'Unnatural Science', *New York Review of Books*, *24*, **1**, pp. 13–18. 3 February.

2 Intelligence and children's development

*Peter Bryant**

There have always been close ties between the devising of ways to measure intelligence and child psychology. The two subjects began at roughly the same time and each at various periods has been directly influenced by advances in the other. These ties are so close and so important that it would be quite hard to understand the twists and turns of the study of intelligence or of children's development without being well versed in both of these topics.

It was like this from the start, which we can put roughly at the first decade of this century. That was when Binet and Simon (1908) devised the first effective intelligence test. Theirs was not the first of these tests: there had been other attempts, most notably Galton's. But Binet and Simon's was the first that really worked and the first, too, to be widely adopted, and one of the main reasons for its success was that it was devised on the basis of data about children.

Binet was a developmental psychologist long before he became an inventor of intelligence tests and he had devised some ingenious ways of showing how striking are the changes in children's ability to remember things and to reason about quantity in general and number in particular. It was he, for example, who first showed how easily children are thrown off course by misleading perceptual cues when they are trying to compare the number of objects in two arrays.

Binet used this early experience of looking at children's development to effect when he began to design his intelligence test. His technique was to include problems in the test only if they were developmentally sensitive—that is to say, only if they turned out to be problems which older children were more likely to get right than were younger children. This simple idea was the key to Binet's success, and it certainly worked. He and Simon assembled an array of problems, from quite easy to very hard ones, and arranged them in such a way that the older children were the greater on the whole was the number

*Watts Professor of Psychology, University of Oxford

of problems that they could solve. It soon emerged that the children who could answer more problems than the average child of their age and thus were in advance for their age were also the children who did particularly well at school. In practical terms the test was a success, for it could predict, and still can, in the relatively short term how well children are likely to cope in an academic situation.

Given the immense success of Binet and Simon's test at the practical level it is easy to forget its considerable effect on developmental theory as well. The truth is that it was the beginning of theories about intellectual development. That was because it showed quite clearly that there is such a thing as intellectual development and thus posed a theoretical question which people have been trying to answer ever since.

Here for the first time was tangible, systematic evidence of intellectual development. The whole process of standardising the test had shown that there are systematic changes in what children are able to do and that these changes are strongly related to age. Furthermore the data from the bottom end of some of these developments were genuinely arresting. Binet and Simon showed that there were some surprisingly simple and basic things which were quite out of the range of very young children. Young children could not remember all that many words read out to them by the tester, they could not say what was wrong with simple and absurd statements like 'Fred's feet were so big that he had to put his trousers on over his head', and they seemed unable to solve some pretty simple logical problems: simple inferences and analogies like 'Arm is to elbow as leg is to . . .' were beyond them at first but came to them as they grew older.

It was this last phenomenon—young children's difficulties with simple problems of logic and reasoning which arrested many people's attention, for it raised an interesting possibility. Could it be that the ability to reason and to understand other people's reasoning was something only gradually acquired through childhood?

In fact this sort of question seems to have brought the great developmental psychologist, Jean Piaget, into the subject. He worked for a while with Simon, Binet's old colleague, and Simon suggested that he try out a new verbal test devised by the ingenious Cyril Burt. Burt's test consisted of a set of logical problems which took the form of a particular kind of deductive inference—the transitive inference. If I tell you that Bill is taller than Fred and Fred taller than Joe, you have at your fingertips not only those two pieces of knowledge, but also the information which follows from them—that Bill is taller than Joe. This A B, B C therefore A C inference involves linking two comparisons about quantity in order to make a third, and it is easy to see that it is a very basic logical move. Unless a child can make it and can understand what is going on when other people make and use such inferences, there is precious little that he or she will understand about quantity and particularly about number. The very idea of ordered number should be out of the range of anyone who cannot reorder the A B, B C comparison into an A B C series.

So, when Piaget (1921) confirmed what Burt had already reported, that young children find such verbal problems extremely difficult and on the whole do not manage to produce the correct answer consistently until the age of eight or nine years, he was able to point out that here was an important theoretical question. Did this mean that children are initially without logic as we know it and spend a great deal of their childhood unable to think or argue logically or to understand logical arguments properly?

His answer is well enough known not to need repeating in detail here. His version of Burt's test was the first in a series of many other tests all of which by and large led to the same general conclusion. Young children, he became convinced, have to acquire logical mechanisms. At first they are virtually without logic of any kind: then during the first two years they build up some kind of a rudimentary system for understanding the world about them but only at a crude and practical level. Only by the age of eight years or so do they become logical in the sense of being able to produce a consciously logical argument, and even that is just a beginning of a process which is not complete until well into adolescence.

It is worth noting that there were really two main statements in Piaget's developmental theory. The first was that children acquire logic slowly as they grow older and the second was about the way they do so. He though that children become logical mainly as a result of informal experiences with their environment, rather than as a result of being told things directly, and he laid great stress on the idea of intellectual conflict. By that he meant that they tend to acquire new ways of thinking when they find that their existing ways produce conflicting answers—in other words, when they find themselves thinking in two different ways about the same thing.

I dwell on Piaget partly because the way his work started is a very good example of the influence of intelligence tests on developmental psychology, partly because this work became such a powerful influence, and partly also because of a rather pronounced similarity between his methods and the methods of intelligence testing. The point that I want to make is that Piaget adopted the single-condition experiment, and that to that extent his methods were like those used to devise intelligence problems. Intelligence tests like Binet's and Burt's consist of a series of problems which children either fail or not. Because each of these problems makes a number of different demands—comprehension, memory, inference, and so on—there is always a number of possible reasons for any failure. That does not matter from the point of view of intelligence tests, because their job is not to provide a reason for failures or successes in the tests, but to make a prediction about a child's or an adult's performance in intellectual-type situations. Of course it is easy when a child solves a problem in a test to say that he has the ability to do X, and when he or she does not to claim that he lacks that ability. But from a theoretical point of view that statement is no more than a description of a result.

Piaget took over the single-condition approach lock, stock and barrel. His long series of experiments, virtually without exception, contain only one task. Of course his account of the children's performance in these tasks is more than just descriptive: it is a genuinely theoretical attempt to get at what children do when they try to solve problems. But the theory was always handicapped by the question marks that are bound to hover around this sort of data.

Most psychological experiments and particularly those whose aim it is to establish whether children are capable of something or not contain more than one condition. They have to, in order to check that successes and failures really are successes and failures in the ability in question. Take, for example, transitive inference. It is easy enough to say that children who succeed have the ability to make transitive inferences and that those who fail do not, and in a way that is right. But what does that mean in the case of the child who fails? He cannot do the task, but that may be for a number of reasons. One is that he is incapable of combining two premises to make a deductive inference, and this presumably would be a genuine logical failure. This is certainly what Piaget suggested is the reason behind the younger children's difficulties with this task. But there were other possibilities: one which we (Bryant and Trabasso 1971) raised some time ago concerns memory: the child may in principle be able to put together two premises to form a new argument, but may not remember them when asked the inferential question. It would have been very easy to have checked for this by asking the child, at the same time as posing the inferential question, to recall the two premises. The failure would only be a genuinely inferential one if he could remember them, but not make the inference.

In fact this particular question has now been the subject of an immense amount of research (Breslow 1981; Thayer and Collyer 1978), and I mention it here only as an example of the consequences of the single-condition approach which was the direct result of the impact of intelligence testing on the methods of developmental psychology. That approach no longer exists, but in some ways we are still living with its consequences, because a great deal of current work on developmental psychology takes the form of a reaction against one aspect of theories based on single-condition experiments. These experiments were bound to exaggerate the incapacities of young children—to be the basis, for example, of claims that children could not make inferences when they might well be able to do so. A large proportion of current research on cognitive development takes the form of showing by means of more sophisticated experiments that young children are not as unskilled as they had been made out to be.

There is a pattern to this second wave of experiments. They tend to consist of two conditions (or more), one of which consists of the old (often Piagetian) paradigm which children find particularly difficult. The other involves some variant of this task which makes the same logical demands but which differs in terms of some other factor (like the amount of remembering involved in the task). Successful experiments of this sort demonstrate that children fail in the traditional task but succeed in the new one, despite the fact that both make the same logical demands. If that happens we have negative evidence against Piaget. But is that all? I think that one can go further, but let us look first at two examples of the sort of experimental result that I have in mind.

One is the well-known experiment by McGarrigle and Donaldson who introduced a new variant of the familiar conservation problem. The conservation task consists of a two-stage problem in which the child sees first two identical rows of counters, judges them to be equal and then one is spread out as the child looks on, and the child is then asked again whether or not the two rows have the same number. McGarrigle and Donaldson's (1974) new variant was to introduce a marauding teddy bear after the first judgement and make it do the spreading of the row as though by accident, and then after putting it away to ask the child to compare the two rows again. The difference between these two conditions was very striking indeed: the children did much better in the teddy bear condition.

The second example is an experiment of our own (Bryant and Kopytynska 1976) on measurement which is often thought to be out of the range of young children because measurement involves the transitive inference. We set the children two closely comparable tasks. In one they were given two identical-looking blocks of wood, each with a hole in the top, and their task was to find out whether these holes were as deep as each other or whether one was deeper than the other. The only way they could do this properly was to use a stick which was also available as a measure. In the other condition the blocks were actually perspex and thus the holes were visible. But we arranged things in such a way that the holes could not really be compared directly with any chance of consistent success because they were physically separate (as were the blocks in the wooden condition). So here again was a task which could only be solved by measuring.

We found that the children measured rather more when given wooden blocks than the perspex ones, and the reason for this seemed very simple. In the perspex condition they resorted to trying to make a direct comparison—to compare the two holes just by looking from one to the other instead of measuring.

What do these experiments have in common? We can start with the most obvious similarity, which is the pattern of success in one condition and failure in a closely similar one. This almost certainly means that the children have the ability in question (to use the principle of invariance, to measure) but do not use it all the time. In that sense both are evidence against some rather negative ideas about children's intellectual abilities. But they are more than that. Both raise the question of why children use an ability or a logical mechanism in one situation but not in another.

The very least that one can say about a pattern of results like this—a pattern which has turned out to be a common one in recent research—is that it suggests that young children are often unsure about when is the best time to use the logical mechanisms that they do possess. They can make inferences, they do know about invariance, but they do not know when exactly to use these inferences and to apply this knowledge. Furthermore the intellectual development involved must be not in straightforward acquisition of these abilities but in the way that they are deployed.

Where, then, does that leave intelligence tests and also the relation between them and developmental psychology? The obvious inference that these tests are not measures of our abilities as such but rather of the way that they are used is not particularly damaging to the value of the tests themselves. After all these are primarily practical tools, tools for predicting academic success, and whether they are picking up information about the existence of a logical skill or about the way that it is deployed is neither here nor there from the point of view of that prediction.

It matters only from the point of view of the theoretical question—what is intelligence and what is intellectual development? It also changes what one thinks of an equally important question, the questions of what causes developmental changes to happen. Intelligence tests demonstrated the existence of huge intellectual changes during childhood but left hanging the question of what prompts them to happen. Piaget and others did produce theories about the causes of these changes, but these were ideas about what causes the acquisition of a skill. Suppose for a moment that I am right and that development is not so much the acquisition of a skill as increasing knowledge about how to deploy it. Then these causal theories would be quite inappropriate because they set about explaining the wrong underlying developmental change.

Let us anyway look at the kinds of theory that have been offered. I have already mentioned Piaget's conflict theory. There is one other important theoretical contender as a possible major cause of intellectual development, and that is language. It is not surprising that a number of psychologists, most notably the Russian psychologists Vygotsky and Luria, thought that the child's linguistic experiences could lead to major changes in the way that he or she understands his environment. It seems a reasonable enough speculation, because so much information can be transmitted through language and because language is an abstract, conceptual system.

These are opposing theories. Piaget disliked the idea that linguisitic communication should be given an important place in intellectual development and was much keener on the idea that the child learns on his or her own through informal experiences with the environment. The linguisitic hypothesis on the other hand stresses the importance of communication, and Vygotsky (1962; 1978) pushed this idea further with his notion of the 'zone of proximal development' which was his idea that there are a lot of things which the child can do only with the help of his or her parents but which later on he will be able to do by himself: the original help leads to the later independence.

For various reasons, the evidence for each of these powerful theories has never been very strong. But here I should like to stick to conceptual arguments, and to make the point that both theories are weakened by conceptual difficulties which make it unlikely that either will provide a complete account of the causes of intellectual development.

Here briefly are the problems. The trouble with Piaget's conflict theory is that it is a mechanism for telling the child that something is wrong but not for letting him or her know what is right. If you find yourself in the uncomfortable position of holding two opposite views on the same subject, you know that at least one of them must be wrong but that is all the conflict could tell you. It does not tell you which is the right one or indeed whether one of them is right at all. It is an incomplete idea; it could not work on its own.

The linguisitic idea is also incomplete, but for quite another reason. There is, as far as I know, no version of this hypothesis which explains the constraints on intellectual development. Whatever it is, it takes a long time. Learning to speak, on the other hand, is accomplished remarkably rapidly. Why then does intellectual development go on for so much longer? If it is just a result of linguistic communication what is to prevent that communication being over in a few judicious tutorials? There is in fact an obvious answer to this complaint. It is that the communication of concepts is no simple matter. There has to be an infrastructure: each new piece of conceptual learning must depend on a great deal of prior learning of supporting concepts, and building this up will take time. A detailed theory about the nature of such an infrastructure would be of very great interest, but so far nobody has produced one.

Is there then an alternative to these two approaches? I should like to offer one which could account for the causes of intellectual development, but only if this development takes the form of children learning to deploy intellectual strategies which are already theirs in principle. This theory, then, explains how children get better at applying strategies and not how they acquire them in the first place. The theory is in fact the opposite of the conflict theory: it is that children learn that a particular strategy is appropriate when they see that it produces the same results as some other strategy. It is the agreement, not the conflict, between strategies which leads to intellectual change.

There is already some evidence for this hypothesis. Very briefly, we have shown (Bryant 1985) that six-year-old children are remarkably reluctant to go through the business of a subtraction sum in order to work out how many counters are left after some have been taken away, even when they are in principle capable of making the subtraction concerned. However, when they are shown that such subtraction sums lead to exactly the same answer as counting the remaining counters afresh—in other words that the two strategies, subtraction and counting, agree—they are much more prepared to subtract in order to solve similar problems. Similarly (Bryant 1982) they begin to measure more when they see that the use of an intervening measure agrees with a direct comparison between the two quantities which are being compared through measurement.

There are several advantages to a theory like this. First, it could work in the way that the conflict theory would not work. If two different strategies consistently produce the same answer, it is really likely that that is the right answer and thus that both strategies are appropriate. But notice that the child must possess these strategies in the first place: this is a theory about how they are used, not how they are acquired.

Secondly, the hypothesis can account for the constraints in development, since linking strategies with each other must take time and anyway is probably dependent to some extent on coincidence. But thirdly, it is the kind of experience which need not just come informally. It is presumably the sort of experience which could be fostered by an adult who appreciates its importance.

I have dwelled on causal theories because it seems to me that they will eventually provide the answer to the theoretical question raised by Binet's test. My idea is that it is foolish to look at the nature of intelligence tests themselves to answer the question. These will only tell you where children are—how far they have got on the intellectual ladder whose existence Binet so brilliantly demonstrated in the first place.

Instead it seems to me that to find the nature of intelligence we should look at the factors which push the children up this ladder, and do so at such startlingly different rates in different children. I have tried to show that one important influence must be the child's ability to spot the connections between different intellectual strategies. In other words I am arguing that part of the essence of intelligence can be found in the relative ability of the young child to build a coherent world for him or herself and to work out the significance of the agreement between different approaches to the same problem.

Developmental psychology owes its existence to the invention of intelligence tests. It seems quite likely to me that it will repay this debt soon by providing a theoretical rationale about the nature of intelligence. That rationale must come from recent discoveries about the causes of development.

References

Binet, A. and Simon, T. (1908), 'Le développement de l'intelligence chez les enfants', *Année Psychologie*, **14**, 1–94.

Breslow L. (1981), 'Re-evaluation of the literature on the development of transitive inferences', *Psychological Bulletin*, **89**, 325–51.

Bryant, P. E. (1982), 'The role of conflict and agreement between intellectual strategies in children's ideas about measurement', *British Journal of Psychology*, **73**, 242–51.

Bryant, P. E. (1985), 'The distinction between knowing when to do a sum and knowing how to do it', *Educational Psychology*, **5**, 207–15.

Bryant, P. E. and Kopytynska, H. (1976), 'Spontaneous measurement by young children', *Nature*, **260**, 773.

Bryant, P. E. and Trabasso, T. (1971), 'Transitive inferences and memory in young children', *Nature*, **232**, 456–8.

McGarrigle, J. and Donaldson, M. (1974), 'Conservation accidents', *Cognition*, **3**, 341–50.

Piaget, J. (1921), 'Une forme verbale de la comparaison chez l'enfant', *Archives de Psychologie*, **18**, 141–72.

Thayer, E. and Collyer, C. (1978), 'The development of transitive inference: a review of recent approaches', *Psychological Bulletin*, **85**, 1327–43.

Vygotsky, L. (1962), *Thought and Language*, Cambridge, MA: MIT Press

Vygotsky, L. (1978), *Mind in Society*, Cambridge, MA: Harvard University Press.

3 Designing intelligence
Daniel C. Dennett*

It is still far too early to ask science for a detailed and non-speculative account of creative intelligence, but that does not leave us without an inkling. We can investigate the question with some more or less controlled speculation, supplementing our biology and psychology with the methods of thought of artificial intelligence. I propose to exhibit a few first steps in this exercise today.

The results will not be so different from what one might get from a traditional philosophical analysis. That is not really surprising, since whatever philosophers may have *claimed* they were doing over the centuries, they have often engaged in just this sort of speculative, aprioristic designing of intelligence, just with a different set of empirical facts and theories, and a less clearly developed or recognised set of design principles.

I will suggest that some familiar features of human reflective consciousness—and the intelligence it makes possible—can be understood as solutions to design problems, solutions arrived at by evolution, but also, in the individual, as a result of a process of unconscious self-design. If we can come to see why a system—or an organ or a behaviour pattern—must have certain features or a certain structure in order to do its task, this may help us ask the right questions, or at least keep us from dwelling on some of the wrong questions, when we try to explain the machinery in the brain that is responsible for intelligent action. 'One of the deepest, one of the most general functions of living organisms is to look ahead, to produce future as Paul Valèry put it' (Jacob 1982, p. 66). Intelligent action in the real world depends on two kinds of anticipation. On the one hand there are the varieties of built-in, fast, unconscious, modular anticipation—the 'unthinking' anticipation tacit in the blinking reflex or the general clutching and squirming that betrays the baby's fear that it is about to be dropped. On the other hand, in the case of human beings and maybe some other higher species, there are the processes of

*Director, Center for Cognitive Studies, Tufts University, USA

voluntary, conscious, expectation formation and calculation about the future.

There is an important family of verbs we use to describe the results of anticipation. Strangely enough this cluster of verbs has not yet been singled out for particular philosophical attention. Central members of the family are *avoid*, *prevent*, *hinder*, *foster*, and, perhaps the most basic of all, *change*, in its transitive sense, where we think of one thing or agent or event 'actively' changing something else. These are the pre-eminent verbs of *action*, where one is characterising the situation in terms of a rational agent who, as one says, sets out to 'change the course of history' (Dennett 1984).

But fully-fledged rational action is just the temporally plastic version of something broader: the designed world of means of *prevention, exploitation* and *protection* that enable living things, while they live, to stand up to the inexorable onslaught of the Second Law of Thermodynamics. The rational agent figures out that if he wants to go on living, he had better step briskly to the left, to avoid the onrushing buffalo; the onrushing twig evokes a swifter and unthinking blink, so as to avoid damage to the eye; the onrushing wind, over a longer, steadier, and more predictable course, evokes a thick coat of fur, so as to prevent undue heat loss. There are reasons for armour plate or for bark, just as there are for sneezing, for eating, for trying to avoid being eaten, and for looking for a better-paid job with a more flexible holiday schedule.

But more relevant to our purposes today than the static heat-loss-avoidance and impalement-avoidance mechanisms such as fur and armour plate, are the swiftly evoked real-time avoidance mechanisms of active and versatile anticipators such as ourselves. Mark Twain once said: 'I'm an old man, and I've seen many troubles, but most of them never happened.' This is the experiential history of somebody who is used to living in the world of avoiding and preventing. This is the world in which a rational deliberator lives. Such a deliberator has to have a world view that is constantly looking forward, anticipating the way things are going to go unless or until it does various things.

How must such a real-time avoider be designed? Suppose, in a thought-experimental mood, that we wanted to design a robot that would live in the real world and be capable of making decisions so that it could further its interests—whatever interests we artificially endow it with. We want, in other words, to design a foresightful planner. How must one structure the capacities—the representational and inferential or computational capacities—of such a being? The problem that such a creature faces is, as usual in artificial intelligence, the problem of combinatorial explosion. The way one obtains anticipations is by sampling the trajectories of things in one's perceptual world and using the information thus gathered to ground an inference or extrapolation about the future trajectory of the thing. One cannot deal intelligently with anything that cannot be tracked in this way. When I speak of tracking, I have in mind not just tracking the trajectories through space of moving things, but also the trajectories through time of things like food stores, seasons, inflation rates, the relative political power of one's adversaries, one's credibility, and so forth. There are indefinitely many things that could be kept track of, but the attempt to track everything, to keep up-to-date information about everything, is guaranteed to lead to a self-defeating paroxysm of information overload. No matter how much information one has about an issue, there is always more that one could have, and one can often know that there is more that one could have if only one were to take the time to gather it. There is always more deliberation possible, so the trick is to design the creature so that it makes reliable but not foolproof decisions within the deadlines naturally imposed by the events in its world that matter to it.

The fundamental problem, then, is what we might call the problem of Hamlet, who, you recall, frittered away his time in deliberation (or so it appears), vacillating and postponing. One has to make decisions in real time, and this means that one has to do a less than perfect job if one is to succeed at all. So one must be designed from the outset to economise, to pass over *most* of the available information.

How, then, does one partition the task of the robot so that it is apt to make reliable real-time decisions? One thing one can do is declare that some things in the world of the creature are to be considered *fixed*; no effect will be expended trying to track them, to gather more information on them. The state of these features is going to be set down in axioms, in effect, but these are built into the system *at no representational cost*. One simply designs the system in such a way that it works well provided the world is as one supposes it always will be, and makes no provision for the system to work well ('properly') under other conditions. The system as a whole operates *as if* the world were always going to be one way, so that whether the world really is that way is not an issue that can come up for determination. The rigid-linkage assumption in human vision described by Ullman (1979) is a good example. It is presumably a design feature endorsed over the aeons by natural selection. In the past, the important things that have moved in our visual neighbourhoods have tended to be assemblages of linkages the parts of which are rigid (hands, wrists, arms, elbows, and so forth), and one can create a much more efficient visual system for a creature with such a world by simply building in the rigidity assumption. This permits very swift calculations for speedy identification and extrapolation of the futures of relevant parts of the world.

Other things in the world are to be declared as *beneath notice* even though they might in principle be noticeable were there any pay-off to be gained thereby. These are things that are not fixed but the changes of which are of no direct relevance to the well-being of the creature. There is often an obvious design trade-off to consider here: should we invest in machinery to notice and respond appropriately to the A-type things, or invest instead in some armour that will render A-type things so harmless to our creature that it can afford to ignore them entirely? (As the immune system demonstrates, the sheer size of the A-type things is not always the issue.) The things that can be ignored with relative safety for one reason or another are smeared into a blur, as it were, in our perceptual world and not further attended to.

An example drawn from Wimsatt (1980) is the difference in cognitive strategy between two different predators: the insectivorous bird and the anteater, which both need to keep track of moving insects. The insectivorous bird tracks individual flying insects and samples their trajectories with a fast sampling technique: a very high flicker fusion rate relative to human vision. (If you showed a motion picture to such a bird, it would see it as a slide show, in effect, not continuous motion.) The bird sees the individual insects *as* individuals. The anteater does not tract individual ants. The anteater sees swarms of ants as batches of edible substance. (If I believed it was always appropriate to speak this way, I would say that 'ant' was a mass term in the anteater's language of thought!) It laps up regions of ant, and does not waste any of its cognitive resources tracking individual ants any more than we track individual molecules when we detect a 'permeating' uniform odour in a volume of air which may contain a few parts per billion of the tell-tale molecule.

The 'grain' of our own perception could be different; the resolution of detail is a function of our own calculus of well-being, given our needs and other capacities. In our design, as in the design of other creatures, there is a trade-off in the expenditure of cognitive effort and the development of effectors of various sorts. Thus the insectivorous bird has a trade-off between flicker fusion rate and the size of its bill. If it has a wider bill it can harvest from a larger volume in a single pass, and hence has a greater tolerance for error in calculating the location of its individual prey.

If, then, some of the things in the world are considered fixed, and others are considered beneath notice, and hence are just averaged over, this leaves the things that are changing and worth caring about. These things fall roughly into two divisions: the trackable and the chaotic. The chaotic things are those things that we cannot routinely track, and for our deliberative purposes we must treat them as random, not in the quantum mechanical sense, and not even in the mathematical sense (for example, as informationally incompressible), but just in the sense of pseudo-random. These are features of the world which, given the expenditure of cognitive effort the creature is prepared to make, are untrackable; their future state is unpredictable.

This means that any real, finite deliberator must partition the states of its world in such a way as to introduce the concept of possibility: it is possible that item n is going to be in state A, and it is possible that item n is going to be in state B, or in state C. We get an ensemble of equipossible (but not necessarily equiprobable) alternatives. This idea of partitioning the world into 'possible' alternatives that remain 'open' is very clearly the introduction of a concept of *epistemic* possibility. It is what is possible relative to a particular agent's knowledge. As the agent gets more knowledge, this may contract the set of possibilities. 'I used to think that state B was possible, but given what I just learned, I realize it is not possible' (Dennett 1984).

Sellars (1963; 1966) draws the very useful distinction between what he calls the manifest image and the scientific image. The manifest image is the everyday world view, the world of macroscopic, solid, coloured objects, and other persons or rational agents. It is the world of folk physics and folk psychology. Then there is the scientific image: the world of atomic and sub-atomic particles too small to be perceived by the naked eye, the world of forces and light waves. Sellars draws his distinction in such a way as to focus on the manifest image shared by (normal) human beings, but I think we can usefully extend his distinction to other species. We are the only species that has developed science, and so we have a scientific image of the world that both we and other species live in, in spite of the vast differences in our manifest images of that world. The manifest image enjoyed by a species is determined, I suggest, by the set of design 'decisions' that apportion things in its environment into the categories of fixed, or beneath notice, or trackable, or chaotic. (It is important to note that this way of thinking of the manifest image of a species somewhat belies the connotations of the adjective 'manifest'—since it presupposes nothing about consciousness. It is not at all ruled out that an 'entirely unconscious' creature—our imaginary robot, for instance —would have a manifest image.)

Why are we the only species to have developed a scientific image in addition to—and somewhat discordant with—our manifest image? That is a topic that has often been written on, so I will pause to make just one point. The principles of design that create a manifest image in the first place also create the loose ends that can lead to its unravelling. Some of the engineering shortcuts that are dictated if we are to avoid combinatorial explosion take the form of ignoring—treating as if non-existent—small changes in the world. They are analogous to 'rounding error' in computer number-crunching. And like rounding error, their locally harmless oversimplifications can accumulate, under certain conditions, to create large errors. Then if the system can notice the large error, and diagnose it (at least roughly), it can begin to construct the scientific image.

For example, we have been designed to detect 'directly' only those changes that occur within a certain speed range. Outside our window of direct visibility lie those changes that happen too fast or too slowly for us to perceive without the aid of time-lapse or slow-motion photography, for instance. We cannot see a plant or a child grow from moment to moment. We can see the sun's motion relative to the earth only at sunrise or sunset, or with the aid of a simple prosthetic extension of our senses—a couple of sticks stuck in the ground will do. But over a few minutes in the latter case, or days or years in the case of plants or children, we detect the difference: our expectations of no change (zero plus zero plus zero . . . equals zero) are overturned. Now the minimal, non-brilliant response to this is simply to make mid-course corrections in our extrapolations of trajectory and continue as before. The insightful response is to notice that we have to do this (often) and to posit *changes too small to be seen*, wedges entering the scientific world of postulated, invisible phenomena. Thus it is from a variety of self-monitoring—in particular the noticing of a pattern in one's own cognitive responses—that the bounteous shift of vision arises.

Let me return to the manifest image of our foresighted planner, with its 'open future' of types of epistemically possible events that matter to it but cannot normally be tracked by it. These are the alternatives it may deliberate about, and must deliberate about if it is to fend for itself in the world. One of the pre-eminent varieties of epistemically possible events is the category of the agent's own actions. These are systematically unpredictable by it. It can attempt to track and thereby render predictions about the decisions and actions of other agents, but (for fairly obvious and well-known logical reasons, familiar in the Halting Problem in computer science, for instance) it cannot make fine-grained predictions of its own actions, since it is threatened by an infinite regress of self-monitoring and analysis. Notice that this does not mean that our creature cannot make some boundary-condition predictions of its own decisions and actions. Thus I can make reliable predictions about decisions I will make in the near future: tomorrow at breakfast I will decide how many cups of tea I will drink, and right now I predict that I will decide to have more than zero and less than four.

Now if our creature is to be able to choose among the alternatives of which it can conceive, with what strategies of deliberation should we endow it? One obvious point: we must guard against the possibility that an evaluation process will end in a tie—the classic problem of Buridan's ass. The cheap way of providing this safety measure is to build in something functionally analogous to a coin-flip: an arbitrary, pseudo-random 'oracle' available for a decision-aiding nudge whenever the system needs it. I am fascinated by Julian Jaynes's (1976) speculation that the various traditions of superstitious decision-making and prognostication found in the ancient world—throwing bones and lots, looking at the entrails of animals, consulting oracles, reading tea-leaves—are actually stratagems more or less unconsciously invented by early human beings in order to get themselves out of the position of Buridan's ass, or out of the somewhat related predicament (Hamlet's, we might say) of one who simply does not know how to deliberate effectively about a complicated situation, and needs nevertheless to act somehow in a timely manner. When the issues are too imponderable, when you can think of no considerations that settle the issue, when you are simply at a loss as to how to continue deliberations, it can be valuable simply to get yourself moving in one direction or another. It doesn't in the long run and on average matter which direction you move as long as you get out of your state of decisional funk and get a move on. These rituals, Jaynes suggests, had the effect of making up people's minds for them when they were not very good at making up their own minds. So these were deliberative crutches, or prostheses. I mention them because they provide a vivid example of something that was not designed and transmitted genetically by natural selection, but rather an artefact, unconsciously designed by individuals and transmitted culturally.

To some ears the phrase 'unconsciously designed' is an oxymoron, but what I mean is quite straightforward: some individuals came haphazardly to engage in these strange behaviours without having any point in mind, but they found they had agreeable results, and so under certain circumstances these behaviours became popular. And so the rituals were subjected to further design refinement and then preserved by cultural transmission.

A behavioural strategy thus transmitted probably has no specific, organic (neural) control system (in computerese, no 'dedicated hardware'), but rather is just software, part of the 'virtual machine' of the human decision-maker shaped by cultural and other environmental factors, and differently implemented in individual control structures.

The computer scientists' concept of a virtual machine is going to prove valuable, I think, in characterising many of the most interesting design features of human intelligence. These features will prove to have a partially cultural and partially personal and idiosyncratic origin, built upon, but not completely determined by, the basic functional organisation of the neural architecture. A virtual machine in computer science is not 'made of hardware' but rather 'made of rules'—made of sets of 'instructions' stored in the computer's memory which, when assiduously followed, lead the actual hardware to 'mimic' the—possibly imaginary—hardware machine that would exhibit just the same behaviour 'because it was wired up that way'. A new virtual machine implemented in a brain would not be made of new fibre bundles or axonal pathways, but of habits of activity that created new regularities of interaction and interdependence.

Suppose, for instance, that one part of the actual neural machinery of a human brain contains some item of information that could be put to good use on certain occasions by a different part of the neural machinery—but suppose there is no 'wire' connecting the two parts in such a way that the information can travel directly between them. A 'virtual wire' might be installed by somehow getting the former part to make public its item of information—render it visible or audible, for instance—so that the other neural part could obtain it by more public routes—by overhearing it, for instance, or seeing it.

Techniques for obtaining this sort of result, wherever it apparently proved valuable, could and would be culturally transmitted under the right conditions. These would be 'ways of using your brain' that did not come entirely naturally, but that could be inculcated, with variations, in developing, learning individuals. As these ways of using a brain became habitual or second nature, they would have the effect of altering the *virtual* functional architecture of those brains—in much the same way a microcomputer acquires a new and different set of competences when one switches from one word processing software to another. Tasks that had been difficult or impossible can become easy and swift; transitions that were previously clumsy become graceful; transformations that were inefficient become efficient, and so forth—all without having to grow any hardware modifications of the neuroanatomy, but just by making many adjustments to the 'habits' of tiny parts of the existing hardware.

Avoiding the gridlock of Buridan's ass is just one design benefit such a virtual machine might provide. Other ways of enhancing the agility of a nervous system depend, as we have seen, on partial monitoring of the system's own behaviour. We must design operating systems that are both simple and efficient enough to avoid combinatorial explosion, while supple and sensitive enough to recover from at least some of the stupid effects of their deliberate oversimplification.

I once had a dog that loved to fetch tennis balls thrown to it, but faced with two balls on the lawn and unable to hold them both in his mouth at once, he would switch rapidly back and forth, letting go of one to grab the other, then seeing the dropped ball, and immediately emptying his mouth again to fetch it, and so forth. He would do this maybe twenty or thirty times, apparently acting on some oversimple rule to the effect that *getting* is better than *keeping*. This was a bad rule more or less built into him—he never unlearned it—but he didn't die of following it. That is, he wasn't so transfixed by the rule that he followed it until he dropped dead of starvation. Something would click over in him after those several dozen iterations and he would stop. He didn't have to know why he stopped. He had a minimal safety valve—somehow sensitive to 'excess' repetition of his own response—that stopped him, and let him set out on some more promising course of action.

A similar case was recently described by Geoffrey Hinton in a talk at MIT on the Boltzmann machine computer architecture he and Terry Sejnowski have developed (Hinton and Sejnowski 1983a; 1983b). Boltzmann machines—so far, only virtual machines simulated on traditional serial computers—are powerful problem-solvers in certain traditionally difficult problem domains, but they have their characteristic weaknesses. Consider a typical problem graphically as the task of finding the lowest spot—the global minimum—in a large terrain dimpled with many depressions—local minima. (This is, of course, just 'hill-climbing' turned upside down.) Boltzmann machines are efficient finders of global minima under many conditions, but they can be trapped in unusual terrains.

Consider a terrain crossed by a steep-sided gully, which slopes gently at the bottom towards the global minimum. When a Boltzmann machine 'enters' such a gully in the course of its explorations, it asks itself, in effect, 'which direction should I go to go down?' and looks around locally for the steepest downgrade. Only at the very bottom of the gully is the gentle slope towards the solution 'visible'; at all other points the fall line (to use skier's jargon) will be at roughly right angles to that direction. With slight overshooting, the Boltzmann machine will end up somewhere on the opposite slope of the gully, ask its question again, and shoot back onto the opposite slope. Back and forth it will oscillate in the gully, oblivious to the futility of its search. Trapped in such an environment, a Boltzmann machine loses its normal speed and efficacy, and becomes a liability to any organism that relies on it.

As Hinton noted on the occasion, what one wants in such a situation is for the system to be capable of 'noticing' that it had entered into such a repetitive cycle, and resetting itself on a different course. The design solution favoured is perhaps not to discard the Boltzmann machine idea because it has this weakness, but to compensate for the weakness with some ad hoc strategy of oversight and management. Just this policy, I think, will be found to be endemic in the design of intelligent control systems.

Suppose we were endowed with some such subsystems in our nervous systems. When faced with the design problem of monitoring the behaviour of such a subsystem, we would not respond by growing some sort of new, internal sense organ to watch, quite literally, the activity of the system. Instead we would figure out some way to get the activity to be monitored to yield a trace that could be detected by one of our existing sense organs. For instance, we would have it 'talk out loud' as it runs through its paces, and then we would listen to what it says, on the alert for the tell-tale signs of vicious looping or other breakdown. Refinements of that crude strategy are, of course, to be expected, and as they developed they would be adopted—unthinkingly—by their beneficiaries, and inculcated—also unthinkingly—in their companions and offspring. Thus different varieties of self-stimulation—talking to oneself, gesturing, sketching, doodling, humming—would emerge and be pruned by selective pressures exerted by the culture and the hard knocks of individual experience.

Out of this process we develop the virtual machines—the 'operating systems'—that get us rather cleverly through life. No doubt there are significant individual differences of style and competence. Strange new mutations of design would irregularly appear, and while many of them would prove to be just strange, a lucky few would prove to be novelties to prize.

These are the creative intelligences: those people—or other organisms, or artefacts—that have hit upon or developed *good* idiosyncratic virtual machines. These virtual machines *tend*, in their heuristic leap into the void of combinatorially explosive possibilities, to notice the right things at the right times—especially the right things about their own activities and operations. They also tend to ignore what can well be ignored. The means by which this especially propitious self-noticing is accomplished would no doubt often appear to be weird and pointless rituals of self-manipulation, but with much 'wasted motion' and baroque filigree, these odd ducks 'use their brains' to surprisingly great effect.

As Buridan's ass learned to its sorrow, literal eccentricity—a certain unbalance—is sometimes the key to making progress. More generally, figurative eccentricities of behaviour are often probably not mere byproducts but sources of creative intelligence, the visible features of opportunistic design tricks that have enhanced the powers of the basic neural machinery. (For further arguments and speculations with similar conclusions, see Hofstadter 1985, esp. ch. 23).

References

Dennett, D. C. (1984), *Elbow Room: the Varieties of Free Will Worth Wanting*, Cambridge, MA: Bradford Books/MIT Press; and Oxford: Oxford University Press.

Hinton, G. and Sejnowski, J. (1983a), 'Optimal Perceptual Inference', *Proceedings of the IEEE Conference on Computer Vision and Pattern Recognition*, Washington, DC, June.

Hinton, G. and Sejnowski, J. (1983b), 'Analyzing Cooperative Computation', *Proceedings of the Cognitive Science Society*, Rochester, NY, May.

Hofstadter, D. R. (1985), *Metamagical Themas: Questing for the Essence of Mind and Pattern*, New York: Basic Books.

Jacob, F. (1982), *The Possible and the Actual*, Seattle: University of Washington Press.

Jaynes, J. (1976), *The Origins of Consciousness in the Breakdown of the Bicameral Mind*, Boston: Houghton Mifflin.

Sellars, W. (1963), *Science, Perception and Reality*, London: Routledge & Kegan Paul.

Sellars, W. (1966), 'Fatalism and Determinism' in K. Lehrer, ed., *Freedom and Determinism*, New York: Random House.

Ullman, S. (1979), *The Interpretation of Visual Motion*, Cambridge, MA: MIT Press.

Wimsatt, W. (1980), 'Randomness and Perceived Randomness in Evolutionary biology', *Syntheses*, **43**, pp. 287–329.

4 Intelligent machines for process control (The 1986 Brunel Lecture)

*Janet Efstathiou**

Introduction

Artificial intelligence (AI) consists of many areas of research, some of which have achieved a certain glamour or notoriety. While most people would be uneasy if a computer replaced their doctor and prefer instead to poke fun at robot barmen and daft machine translation programs, AI is being applied in many areas of industry, in a quiet advance in the automation of tasks that hitherto only humans could accomplish.

The industrial applications of which people may be aware are things like robot paint-sprayers in car factories, voice recognition for secure installations, natural language interaction with computers and databases and the ability to recognise features and objects in a picture, or to read handwriting. To the man on the Clapham omnibus, the performance of some of these sophisticated computer programs would be very unimpressive indeed, since most four-year-olds could do a better job of understanding speech and handprinted characters. However, AI techniques are important and useful, because although humans are unequalled for inventiveness and flexibility, when a computer applies a very small amount of intelligence in a consistent way very quickly without getting bored, then the resulting behaviour can be impressive.

Many of the AI techniques mentioned above are useful and have been applied in industry, such as the robot paint-sprayers and automatic vision systems to detect faulty products. But this paper will concentrate on the construction and application of expert systems and intelligent knowledge-based systems (IKBS). Such systems have been proposed as adjuncts or assistants in the application of human skills, such as advising on the design of an automatic controller or in improving on a designer's layout for a microchip. But we shall

*Lecturer, Department of Electrical and Electronic Engineering, Queen Mary College, University of London and the 1986 Brunel Lecturer.

concentrate on systems capable of performing tasks of a magnitude and complexity beyond that which humans could ever tackle. Computer techniques are already being used in these areas, but we will argue for a unified approach, with modest amounts of intelligence applied over and over again to bring about improvements in industrial performance and safety.

Expert systems are becoming well established through practice in industrial process control, with many applications in the areas of low-level control and fault diagnosis. However, although these techniques have had some success, their capabilities are being limited by the essentially piecemeal approach to construction and installation. We recommend an intelligent knowledge-based system, which would be a suite of computer programs, operating upon a collection of data structures represented within the computer, and with access to sensors attached to the processes which are to be managed. The combination of special-purpose hardware and software would comprise an intelligent machine.

This chapter will describe the developments in AI and the requirements of process control which could be brought together in the intelligent machine. The next section will review some recent applications of expert systems in the broad area of process control, concentrating on the rule-based methods of knowledge representation. Then follows an outline of the tasks of control, from controlling low-level processes to planning and designing entire production plants. The kinds of knowledge and inference that are required for each level of activity will also be described, showing the continuity between what are often considered distinct tasks.

Thereafter, we concentrate on the kinds of knowledge and inference technique that would be required to produce a unified approach to process control. We introduce the concept of a frame, which may be regarded as a complex data structure for representing knowledge within a computer, and show how this has been used to create models of simple process plant. Finally, we describe the hardware and software requirements of the intelligent machine, suggesting that such a machine could be constructed within the next decade.

Expert systems and intelligent knowledge-based systems

Expert systems have been one of the most popular and widespread applications of AI. The earliest expert systems were developed about fifteen years ago at Stanford in California, for application in medical diagnosis and mineral prospecting (Shortliffe 1976; Hart *et al.*, 1978). Since then, the techniques have developed markedly and relatively sophisticated expert-system software (called shells) to run on industry-standard personal computers can be bought for £500 or less.

The purpose of an expert system is to enable a novice in a particular domain of human expertise to emulate the behaviour of an expert problem-solver (see Figure 4.1). Experts are very busy people and have acquired their skills through many years of training and expertise. During the years, they may have encountered some unusual and rare cases, which might not have been recorded any-where, although the expert may remember what to do. Transmitting this kind of experiential knowledge to the next generation can not always be done efficiently, so that an organisation may be doomed to repeating the same mistakes while the new experts learn.

Figure 4.1 Using a rudimentary expert system, and how it is per-ceived by computer and novice user. The computer guides the novice's behaviour as if he had an expert adviser, while the representation within the computer is of an inference engine program, operating upon a separate knowledge-base.

An expert-system computer program records the knowledge of experts in a knowledge-base. The knowledge-base may be updated and amended as new knowledge is acquired. It serves as a repository of the knowledge of the experts, and may be used for solving real problems or as an aid to training new experts. The construction of an expert system may be the first occasion when the informal knowledge of the organisation has been gathered together in one place, in a well-formulated manner.

Many computer programs aim to assist people to solve problems or make decisions, but the distinguishing feature of expert systems is the dichotomy between the knowledge in the knowledge-base and the program which manipulates it, called the inference engine. The inference engine may be available as a shell. This dichotomy means that if the knowledge needs to be changed, the knowledge-base alone can be edited, which is a very quick and simple thing to do. If the knowledge and the program for manipulating it had been incorporated into one program, then amending the knowledge would be much more difficult, because locating the part of the program which needed changing could be a problem in practice, and the whole program might need to be recompiled, which adds up to a much more time-consuming and error-prone process.

Industrial applications of expert systems

We shall consider two main areas where expert systems have been successfully applied in industry, i.e. in process control and fault diagnosis.

Process control

Modern control theory has achieved important advances in the quality of control of many industrial processes, but a few processes remain which for various reasons have been more difficult to solve, for example the manufacture of cement. The process of converting raw materials mined from the earth into cement clinker within a cement kiln is not well understood, because of the complex chemical reactions at high temperatures within the kiln and the difficulty of controlling the quality of the raw materials supplied. However, cement of an adequate quality can be produced by leaving the control of the kiln to skilled human operators, or experts.

Unfortunately, cement kilns are run twenty-four hours a day, and so several shifts of operators are needed. Some operators are better than others, so the quality of produce fluctuates. Also, operators have a tendency to play safe and run the kiln at a higher operating temperature than required, increasing the energy consumption and, therefore, the expense of cement manufacture.

Expert systems are now being used to represent the operators' control strategy, so that an automatic controller can reproduce the behaviour of the best human operators. Note that the controller works by reproducing the behaviour of the operator, and not by using a detailed chemical model of the process of cement manufacture.

Such systems are now sold as standard equipment by the Danish company F.L. Smidth, who manufacture and install cement-manufacturing plant. These expert-system controllers have been installed throughout the world and have been found to need very little tuning to the specific conditions of each site. Blue Circle in the UK are investigating expert-system controllers and have installed them successfully at several sites in this country. The research and development company, Sira, have developed a complete system tailored to the needs of the process-control industry. General purpose rule-based controllers are now sold by at least two Japanese companies, and GE in the USA are working on a single-chip version of the controller. The expert-system controllers are based on fuzzy logic and were first devised in 1974 by Prof. E. H. Mamdani at Queen Mary College (see Mamdani 1974).

Fault diagnosis

The other main area of application of expert systems which we shall discuss is fault diagnosis. Production lines consist of many different pieces of equipment, for mixing, heating, storing, cooling, shaping or wrapping material. It is often the case that the fitters who repair equipment may develop special expertise on one particular kind of machine. Sometimes, only one individual might have the knack of getting a particular machine to work properly, and when he is on a different shift or on holiday, then the efficient running of the whole production line may be affected. If such an expert can be persuaded to explain to someone else how he makes his decisions, then that knowledge can be stated formally and represented in an expert system. The form that the knowledge often takes is:

IF ⟨situation⟩ THEN ⟨action⟩

for example, IF ⟨the chocolate is runny⟩ THEN ⟨check that the oven temperature is not above 200°C⟩.

Expert systems using knowledge of this kind may be used to discover quickly what has gone wrong on the production line. This means that a repair can be made more quickly, reducing plant down-time and making more effective use of the factory's resources. A well-known example is Delta, an expert system used by GE in the USA to diagnose faults on diesel locomotives. Once the fault has been identified, the expert system guides the repairman as to how to replace the faulty component, using videodisc equipment.

Constructing expert systems

The expert controller and fault diagnosis expert-system as described both rely on an expert who can provide the knowledge. The expert's knowledge is a very important asset to the organisation and a computer program may be a more secure vessel for such valuable knowledge than a fragile human head.

However, there are some disadvantages with expert systems of this kind. First of all, the expert may be very busy and might not have the time to provide the knowledge or to make sure that it is correct. Secondly, if the expert has not provided a rule about what to do in a particular situation, the expert system might not be able to respond, or might give its next best, possibly wrong answer. Further, such an expert system may be inflexible because it has been constructed with a particular set of equipment in mind, and the local rules of thumb might not apply to a similar plant elsewhere. Therefore, the whole system would have to be constructed all over again for another plant or even if the original plant were altered in some way, perhaps by removing or installing another component.

It is also important to note that the activities of fault diagnosis and control are not unrelated. When a plant disturbance occurs, the controller responds by attempting to restore the process output to the desired set point. It may be the case that a fault has developed somewhere, so that instead of recovering from the disturbance, it grows worse and the controller cannot cope. At this point a fault maybe suspected and the fault diagnoser may take over. The transition from control to fault diagnosis is achieved via alarm monitoring, that is, checking that process outputs and operating conditions have not exceeded acceptable levels. It would be useful if the fault diagnoser had access to the sequence of actions that the controller had already taken, since information on the rate of development and history of the fault could narrow down the set of possible suspects.

Unfortunately, at the moment, expert systems for process control and fault diagnosis are not linked together. The knowledge-bases are quite separate, and indeed the inference engines that are used may be different. This is partly a consequence of relying upon experts as the source of knowledge.

However, systems can be constructed that do not require the heuristic, experiential knowledge of experts. In order to emphasise this distinction, we shall reserve the term 'expert system' for systems that contain the knowledge of experts in the knowledge-base. Systems that retain the distinction between inference engine and knowledge-base will be referred to as knowledge-based systems (KBS). An expert system is, therefore, an example of a knowledge-based system. If a KBS is provided with inference techniques that enable it to carry out extra activities so that it can derive new knowledge or learn, then we shall call it an intelligent knowledge-based system (IKBS). We will return to the kinds of knowledge and inference technique that would be required in process control in a later section.

The tasks of industrial control

The previous section introduced the technology of expert systems and IKBS, with examples drawn from process control. It was pointed out that there are links between the activities of low-level control and fault diagnosis, but that current expert systems have not been designed to take this into account. Before examining an extended role for IKBS in industrial control, it is worthwhile looking in a little more detail at the scope of activities within control.

As we have already discussed, the lowest level of control consists of managing a process which takes material inputs, applies some change to them and endeavours to maintain the process output within specified limits around a set point. Minor fluctuations in the operating environment or quality of the inputs may be coped with by the controller, which will take corrective action so as to restore the process output to the setpoint. Typically, control actions at this level may be needed as often as every few milliseconds or only once an hour, as with the cement kiln.

When the plant disturbances are more drastic or a fault develops, the controller cannot cope. The plant operator may summon assistance or an automatically monitored system may indicate an alarm. At this stage a different kind of expertise may be involved. The experienced diagnostician would observe the state of the plant and make a few guesses about what could have gone wrong. Some faults may be more common than others, so it would be sensible to check them first. A few extra tests may be required to identify exactly the fault or faults.

In order to carry out the diagnostic task, the expert might need to look at other pieces of equipment located physically near to the source of the alarm or which may be responsible for supplying its input or drawing off the output. Whereas low-level process control requires little more than awareness of a single vessel and its associated sensors, fault diagnosis requires knowledge of the interconnected pieces of plant. The time-scale of fault diagnosis could typically range from a fault developing on a particular piece of equipment about once every hour to once a year or more. A fitter might diagnose and repair a dozen or so faults a day.

In selecting tests to distinguish between candidate faults, the fitter needs to know more than just which machines are associated with each other, but also how they behave. For example, adjusting a valve setting at one point should be indicated by a change in a sensor here and an alteration in the appearance of material x there. Given knowledge of interconnections and behaviours, it is a short step to reconfiguring the plant to avoid or cure faults. For example, if a blockage is building up in a pipe, then increasing the input pressure could clear the blockage. Alternatively, knowing the alternative pathways through the plant means that the faulty piece of piping could be avoided and shut off for replacement. Realistically, the fitter might not have responsibility for altering the state of the plant in this way, but his suggestion could be implemented by a plant scheduler.

Scheduling is the activity of allocating tasks to different components within the plant. For example, a paint shop could have many different paint sprayers, with a set of car bodies to paint in different colours. The scheduler's job is to ensure that the bodies are painted in the required colours, but minimising the number of changes of paint colour for each sprayer, because colour changes mean time is lost while the new colour moves through the sprayer. Formal techniques exist for drawing up optimised schedules, but these need to be adapted quickly by the scheduler in response to equipment breaking down, staff falling sick or urgent jobs coming in.

The scheduling activity also requires knowledge about the interconnections between plant components, and historical data about the frequency of breakdown and length of down-time would also be useful. Scheduling is often done once a week, but adjustments to the schedule may be required several times a day.

The next highest level of activity is planning, occurring at the longest time-scale. Again, the time-scale can vary enormously, but would typically be monthly to once every few years, depending on the complexity of the system being managed. Planning is another activity that has received plenty of attention within AI. An important approach to planning proceeds by formulating an overall plan and refining each step to ever greater levels of detail. Ultimately, the plans could come down to the level of schedules.

Planning means making long-term decisions about the role of the plant in a wider context, within the external environment of the local economy and markets. Decisions will not only be about the quantity of different products to manufacture, but will also concern the fabric of the plant itself, such as the necessity to shut down, reopen or extend parts of the plant. In these circumstances, skilled designers may be needed who can design a plant to fulfil certain production requirements, but paying attention to costs, reliability and safety. Many possible designs could be conceived, but their flexibility for scheduling, reliability for maintenance and ease of process control all need to be considered.

A unified model-based approach to process control

Knowledge and inference

So far, in the previous section, we have looked at the broad sweep of activities that fall within process control, from long-term planning to rapid process control. The time-scales involved have been indicated, but next we should turn to the kinds of knowledge and inference technique that would be required. Again, we shall begin at the lowest level of process control and argue from there (see Table 4.1).

We have already indicated that low-level process control can be achieved by using a knowledge-base which consists of IF ⟨situation⟩ THEN ⟨action⟩ rules. These rules cope with the complexity of the process in the same manner as the human operators, that is, by applying experience. The inference technique required could hardly be simpler. By reading the sensors, the controller determines the state of the plant. This is compared in turn with the antecedent (IF) part of the rules until a match is found. At that point, the consequent

Table 4.1. The range of activities covered by industrial process control

Activity	Time-scale	Kinds of knowledge	Kinds of inference	Linked on
Low-level control	milliseconds to hours	Process	Forward chaining	
Fault diagnosis	hours to years	Process & plant	Forward chaining Backward chaining Qualitative simulation Hypothesis list management Test generation	Alarm monitoring
Scheduling	weekly	Plant	Constraint matching Constraint specification Schedule generation Schedule critiquing Justification	Plant re-configuration
Planning design	years	Process & plant	Simulation Critiquing Parts list generation Risk assessment	Refinement of plans
economic	years	Process (external) world	Simulation What-if scenario generation Critiquing Plan refinement	
Training		Process & plant	Critquer Explainer all of the above	

(THEN) part of the rule is invoked. This may recommend an adjustment to a fuel or material input.

So, low-level process control deals in process complexity, using IF ⟨situation⟩ THEN ⟨action⟩ rules and simple forward chaining as the inference technique.

Fault diagnosis requires knowledge of the interconnections of the components of the plant, that is to say, some knowledge of plant complexity. By recognising the state of the plant, the KBS could generate a list of possible faults, or hypotheses. IF ⟨situation⟩ THEN ⟨action⟩ rules could still be used, but here the action would be 'suspect component x'. In deciding which component to check, the same kinds of rules could be used, but applied in the other direction, so that we could look for other rules concerning component x as the consequent and then checking if the situation in the IF part is confirmed. This would lend support to the original hypothesis that component x was at fault. This kind of inference is called backward chaining, because we look from consequent to antecedent.

At this level, IF ⟨situation⟩ THEN ⟨action⟩ rules can be applied, but a mixture of forward and backward reasoning would help. Process knowledge is less important, but plant knowledge is becoming necessary. The increasing role of plant complexity has a major impact on the knowledge-base. Because of the importance of plant complexity, we shall postpone the discussion of scheduling and planning until after an explanation of modelling and plant complexity.

Modelling plant complexity

In order to diagnose faults, the experienced fitter looks at surrounding and related pieces of equipment. These activities could be represented as rules, but another data structure lends itself more readily to this kind of approach—the frame.

Frames were first suggested by Marvin Minsky (1975) of MIT. They are collections of data organised in a way that is supposed to resemble the way humans store information, with all the knowledge about particular objects stored together. Frames also tend to be organised as a hierarchy, so that properties can be inherited by frames lower down the hierarchy. Frames differ from simple data records because procedures can also be associated with the 'slots' of the frame.

Figure 4.2 shows an inheritance hierarchy for plant components. The general properties of all components are represented at 'Com-

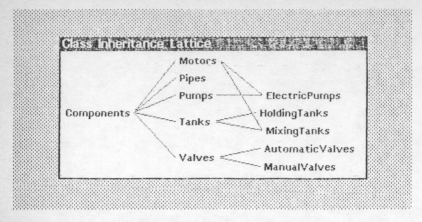

Figure 4.2 A sample hierarchy of industrial plant components.

ponents'. These are inherited by 'Motors', 'Pipes', 'Pumps', 'Tanks' and 'Valves'. Two kinds of 'Valves' exist, 'AutomaticValves' and 'ManualValves', which have different properties, but both inherit from 'Valves'. Note that there are two kinds of 'Tanks'. 'Holding-Tanks' inherit properties from 'Tanks' alone, but 'MixingTanks' inherit from 'Tanks' and 'Motors', because a motor is used to turn the mechanism which mixes the contents of the tank.

The hierarchy describes general class properties of components, but a mechanism is needed to represent the properties of individual components of the plant. Figure 4.3 depicts the frame for a particular component, called PumpA, with the default settings of the slots. Note that the first two slots are called 'component-Input' and 'component-Output'. Values inserted here would help construct a model of the interconnections of the plant. For example, placing 'TankD' as componentInput and 'TankA' as componentOutput would enable the KBS to generate automatically a plan of the plant (see Figure 4.4).

These diagrams were devised and programmed by Dr Costas Koukoulis (1986) for his PhD thesis on KBS in industrial mainten-ance. The computer used was a Xerox 1108, using the LOOPS object-oriented programming environment.

Now, we have an alternative data structure—the frame. An enormous degree of flexibility becomes available in what may be included in the frame, but in the first place, we can see how a model of the plant's complexity could be constructed by specifying the

Pump Components

```
All Values of ElectricPumps SPumpA
componentInput      NIL
componentOutput     NIL
inFlow              #(((Normal 0 Default))
                       GETHISTORY PUTLASTHISTORY)
lastinFlow          (Normal 0 Default)
outFlow             #(((Normal 0 Default))
                       GETHISTORY PUTLASTHISTORY)
lastoutFlow         (Normal 0 Default)
intemp              NIL
outtemp             NIL
inPressure          #(((Unknown 0 Default))
                       GETHISTORY PUTHISTORY)
outPressure         #(((Unknown 0 Default))
                       GETHISTORY PUTHISTORY)
faultStatus         #(((Ok 0 Default))
                       GETHISTORY PUTLASTHISTORY)
lastfaultStatus     (Ok 0 Default)
workingStatus       #(((On 0 Default))
                       GETHISTORY PUTLASTHISTORY)
lastworkingStatus   (On 0 Default)
```

Figure 4.3   The frame for PumpA.

components' inputs and outputs. Rules and frames are not incompatible or mutually exclusive. It is perfectly reasonable that rules about controlling classes of component are included within the frame. Rules and frames each have their good and bad points and the IKBS designer will choose how their use should be determined.

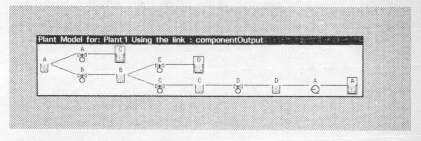

Figure 4.4   A computer-generated layout of the plant.

To return to the activity of maintenance, we have found that models of this kind are used by fault diagnosis experts. Commonly occurring faults are diagnosed by rules of thumb of the IF ⟨situation⟩ THEN ⟨action⟩ type, but infrequently occurring faults are diagnosed by the diagnoser referring to a logical model of the plant which the diagnoser understood. On one occasion, we were trying to capture the diagnostic knowledge of two expert designers. In contrast to fitters who worked on the plant every day, the designers relied very heavily upon a conceptual model of the plant. When questioned about a particular situation, their response was to apply that to their mental model and reason from first principles what the effects would be. It seemed more efficient to try to capture and manipulate their model than try to get them to exercise it and express the outcome as rules.

The ability to construct models of this kind has several advantages. We have already pointed out that expert systems can fail if rules for particular situations are not supplied. If a model exists, then the model could simulate the behaviour of the plant and predict what would happen. This kind of behaviour would mean that the KBS was generating knowledge that it had not originally been told explicitly, so a KBS with that capability could be designated intelligent, according to the definition at the end of the first section of this chapter.

We have also noted already that expert systems do tend to be inflexible, because the rules have to be altered if the configuration of the plant changes. Adding or removing components from the plant can be handled by modifying the componentInput and component-Output slots for particular components. Thus, automatic plant reconfiguration can be accommodated.

With a rule-based system, there may be doubt about whether the collection of rules is complete. If a model were constructed, with a limited number of components and a limited number of classes of fault, it would be possible to generate a complete description of the situations which would be observed when each of all possible faults arose. The rules obtained in this way could be summarised and represented more efficiently by using induction. In so doing, KBS would again be manifesting something very like intelligence, by generating knowledge that it had not originally obtained, particularly so if it produced a rule that the experts had not considered.

The role of models in process control

We shall resume the discussion of knowledge representation and inference, with the additional possibility of a more suitable representation of plant complexity. Fault diagnosis may now be tackled in either of two ways. Either rules may be tried to see if the observed situation is adequately covered by any of the known rules, or the model of the plant could be exercised to see if the observed situation can be simulated. The second is the approach investigated in Koukoulis's thesis.

Rather than specifying all possible faults that could occur on a plant, it is more reasonable to look at the kinds of fault that could occur on classes of component. For example, pumps could develop leaks or total or partial blockages. If the IKBS knows the component that has detected the developing fault, then immediately the number of possible faulty components can be limited to those reasonably nearby. For example, we might include PumpA in the list of possible candidates. Since there are three kinds of fault that inflict pumps, we could reasonably suggest that PumpA is leaking or has a partial or total blockage. Thus, we could generate three possible worlds, each containing one fault. These three worlds could be run forward together, comparing them with the real plant. Eventually, some of the candidate faults will show up as bearing little resemblance to the observations, so that they could be deleted from the list. With luck, one candidate will match observations so closely that it will be an obvious explanation of the fault. More likely, several possibilities may suggest themselves as being roughly equal. At this stage several possible techniques exist to resolve the contest between them. If qualitative simulation only has been used, quantitative techniques could be used, taking advantage of the numerical information that may be available from the sensors. Or tests could be generated.

Qualitative simulation is another area of AI which is currently receiving attention (Kuipers 1985). It is a technique which models the behaviour of physical systems by examining the qualitative changes that occur during a process. As an example, the qualitative changes which are of interest in modelling a bouncing ball occur each time the ball changes direction that is, when it strikes the ground or reaches the peak of its bounce (see Figure 4.5).

Qualitative simulation is not concerned with detailed mathematical models, and many simulations rely on a three-valued logic, where zero, greater than zero and less than zero may be the only values of interest. The rates of change of values may also be included. The lack of mathematical detail means that the qualitative aspects of the model may be simulated by the computer very quickly, giving an advantage over mathematical models. However, the lack of numerical detail does mean that the simulation could not distinguish between

(a)

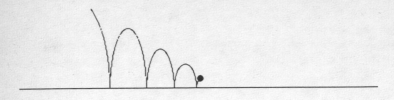

(b)

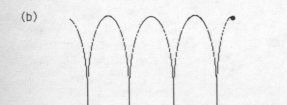

(c)

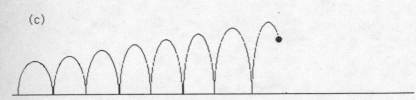

Figure 4.5　Qualitative simulation can model a bouncing ball (a), but it cannot detect that a ball which always bounces to the same height (b), or which gaines height with each bounce (c), cannot exist.

the validity of a model where a ball kept bouncing to the same height or even gained height with each bounce. The extra inference techniques that would be required to accompany a model to achieve fault diagnosis might be: qualitative simulation; automatic data acquisition; situation assessment; hypothesis list management; test generation.

Scheduling has less interest in process complexity, but could make great use of a plant model. If the frames contained slots describing the capacity of throughput of the component then, when provided with a set of requirements, the IKBS could generate a possible schedule. However, the human scheduler may be aware of temporary disturbances and might want to add extra constraints to the scheduling program, so that particular machines were not so heavily loaded or an important order was fulfilled early. Thus, the scheduler should be able to amend the computer-generated schedule and have the IKDS generate a new one. Once a schedule was implemented, automattic sensors could detect that the schedule is being filled as required or alert the program to impending difficulties on the equipment. If pre-emptive orders come in, the scheduling program would have to adjust again.

The programs surrounding the model would now have to include a schedule generator and constraint matcher; constraint specifier; schedule critiquer; justifier. We add a schedule critiquer and justifier because, at this level of decision-making, the interaction between user and machine has a mixed initiative. We would suppose that the user might want to propose a schedule and have the machine assess it and provide an account of why it considers it to be less than optimal, that is what is often called critiquing. Similarly, when the machine proposes its own schedule, the user would want to know why the machine considers it to be so good. This can help show up the validity of the constraints under which the schedule generator is operating.

When planning involves setting the plant within the economic environment, the executive decision-maker will need a model of the environment. Few satisfactory economic models seem to exist, so again, process models might be required, based on the same sort of IF ⟨situation⟩ THEN ⟨action⟩ rules as were used at the bottom level of process control. But situation assessment is a different problem now, because reliable, scientific sensors do not exist. This problem is usually handled by having the decision-maker postulate a situation and predicting how specified plans would fare under those circumstances. In this way a plan can be generated that might be robust under several different scenarios. This is sometimes referred to as 'what-if' decision-making.

The other aspect of planning is the design and modification of the plant. The designer may want to specify several different layouts of the plant and consider how each would perform in terms of construction costs, fault propagation, running costs and flexibility. This could be done by providing the designer with a library of components, covering all the pumps, tanks, valves, ovens, wrapping machines, and so on, that the organisation uses, and thereby enabling the designer to link instances of the components together to form a model of the plant. If the frames contain details of the parts which form a component and their costs, then suitable programs could generate a shopping list of parts. Using simulators similar to those used in diagnosis, the designer could postulate the existence of faults and assess their likely effects, or hand over some initiative to the machine and have it look for possibly catastrophic faults. For this procedure to be useful in practice, the model of the plant would need to run much faster than real time, so that an acceptable speed of response is provided to the designer.

We have already mentioned briefly the usefulness of expert systems for training novice experts. Once constructed, the IKBS could be modified by adding extra interfaces so that a trainee could learn from an endlessly patient and always available teacher. For example, if we look again at fault diagnosis, when an alarm is detected, the fitter wants a diagnosis of the fault with instructions on the repair action as quickly as possible. We could call this the 'what now?' mode. Once the panic has died down, the fitter could return to the IKBS and ask for a detailed explanation of how the machine combined observations with its process and plant knowledge to generate a conclusion, the 'why this?' mode. Further, the fitter might have had another idea about what could have gone wrong and would like to know why that explanation had been rejected by the IKBS. The fitter could supply her own explanation for comparison with the machine's diagnosis, observing the progression of the parallel simulations and obtaining an explanation of the similarities and differences of the two diagnoses, the 'why not this?' mode. The design and construction of a mixture of interfaces such as these for a fault diagnosis IKBS is the subject of Soheir Ghallab's PhD research. See Table 4.1 for a summary of these points.

The architecture of the intelligent process-control machine

Figure 4.1 depicted the simplest possible knowledge-based system, with a knowledge-base separate from the program which manipulates it. In this example, data from the outside world are obtained via a keyboard. Figure 4.6 depicts a much more complex IKBS for process control. Again, the knowledge-base is separate, but is now structured as a hierarchy of classes, with a large range of knowledge held for each class. Instead of just one user interface, there are now several, as well as a host of connections to external sensors and other computers. We shall discuss the physical architecture of the intelligent machine in terms of the sensors, central processor and the user interface terminals.

Sensors

Sensing equipment is crucially important. We have emphasised throughout that the IKBS should be able to respond in real time, that is, at a speed no less than that at which real events occur. Real-time operation would not be possible if the IKBS relied upon human operators typing in all information via a keyboard. Indeed, the success of the expert controllers for cement kilns was partly due to improvements in sensing technology, because data could now be acquired automatically that had hitherto depended on operators to recognise.

The data which the sensors gather are used to control particular pieces of equipment. These data would be compared against control rules and control actions generated. For a complex plant, it might not be feasible for all the raw data to be passed to a central processor, which is responsible for calculating the control actions for every individual piece of equipment. If a fault were to develop on that single processor, then the whole plant would shut down.

Instead, each major component of plant would have its own onboard computer, which could serve two purposes. The main purpose is to generate control actions and maintain process output to acceptable levels. The other purpose, proceeding in the background, is to gather statistical data, logging the output of the process, the control actions, and so on. These statistical data would be passed to the next level of processing when a fault is detected and the controller can no longer cope, that is, as an alarm is triggered.

A third possible purpose for the onboard computer is to do some simple fault diagnosis itself, by looking for patterns in the behaviour of the sensors, which might indicate a fault in the controller or the component, for example.

Alternatively, the computing power could be distributed yet further, by putting a microprocessor within the sensor, so that, when it detects a trend towards unacceptable levels, it passes a message to its mother computer, which responds by looking at the states of other sensors. This could be used as a way of detecting faults in the sensors themselves. Thus, we could have smart sensors which are self-monitoring.

This processing power within the sensors need not be very special at all. A straightforward circuit with a few chips could do the job. The onboard computer which receives data from the sensors could be stand-alone, in that it would not need to be connected to the central processor to operate successfully. It need not be a very sophisticated computer either—BBC micros have already been used for this purpose.

Central processor

Throughout this chapter, we have referred to the importance of time, so one overriding requirement of the system is that is should operate in real time, that is, the model should run at least as quickly as the real plant. There is little point in its being slower, since events would soon overtake it. There are other requirements that also dictate the design of the IKBS. One is that it should be safe, so that if a fault develops on the processor, the operation of the plant is not in jeopardy. Also, if a fault occurs on the plant, it should be detected and diagnosed as quickly as possible, before dangerous consequences occur. Apart from reliability and safety, the whole system should be capable of being installed in easy stages and on existing plant. Thus, a plant manager might decide to install only smart sensors and no higher intelligence than that, or could decide to install the whole range from control to planning but only on a very narrow range of components. Therefore, the main requirements are speed of operation, reliability and flexibility of installation.

These requirements suggest the use of a highly distributed architecture, so that the computing activities are shared amongst many small processors. A single, central processor to handle all the control tasks would be vulnerable, would need to be able to accept many thousands of sensor inputs, should be capable of fast symbolic and mathematical computation, would be expensive to buy and would need to be carefully backed up with an auxiliary processor of equivalent power to ensure continuous operation. Another advantage of a distributed architecture is that the processor can be tailored to the task it is selected to perform. So, when numerical computation is needed, as on the onboard computers, the appropriate processor is chosen, but when symbolic computation is needed, as for qualitative modelling, then a processor designed for that kind of purpose could be used.

A central processor is still needed, therefore, but if much of the processing is devolved to computers closely attached to the components, then the amount of computation required from the central processor is greatly reduced. Also, the system can be introduced gradually, and enhanced in terms of sensing or central computation as required.

User interface terminals

Aside from receiving and transmitting signals to sensors and controllers, the IKBS must also interact with people, who will be using the IKBS in many different ways through the various interfaces and in many different locations, from the peaceful, clean conditions of the research laboratory to the noisy, dusty environment of the control room.

Therefore, it is important that the terminals are designed to reflect these differences in use. The controller's terminals might have only a small number of keys or be voice operated (where possible) to keep dust out. For fault diagnosis, it might be necessary for the terminal to be light and portable, so that the fitter can carry it around while patrolling the plant. The designer's terminal, on the other hand, can remain fixed in one place, which means that a much more sophisticated display can be used, with colour displays of models of the plant in operation, and several tasks proceeding in parallel. Non-technical or executive staff would need a terminal which is simple and pleasant to use, with the minimum of typing and using menus and icons wherever possible.

Other user-interface enhancements are possible. The IKBS could construct a model of the person who is interacting with it at any time, based on their use of the programs, speed of response, etc, allowing the IKBS to assess the user's familiarity with the system and expectations from it.

The mixed initiative programs used by designers and trainees should also operate at acceptable rates, since a user will quickly grow frustrated and bored if having to wait more than a few seconds for a response from the machine, underlining the importance of speed of operation.

Figure 4.6 depicts the conceptual arrangement of the intelligent machine, and Figure 4.7 suggests a possible physical arrangement.

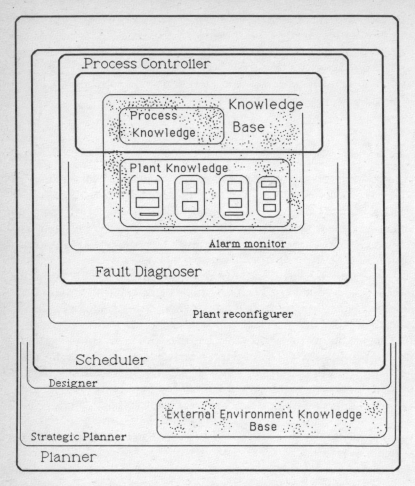

Figure 4.6 A conceptual model of the IKBS for process control.

Feasibility

To assess the design of the IKBS outlined above, one should consider
both the hardware and the software. The trend in hardware design
has been for processors to become cheaper and smaller. Special
purpose AI machines are now available from many companies, with
central processors designed to achieve speed in symbolic computation. By distributing the intelligence, we minimise the processing
effort required of the central processor, so that the machines which
exist today could probably achieve what has been outlined above.

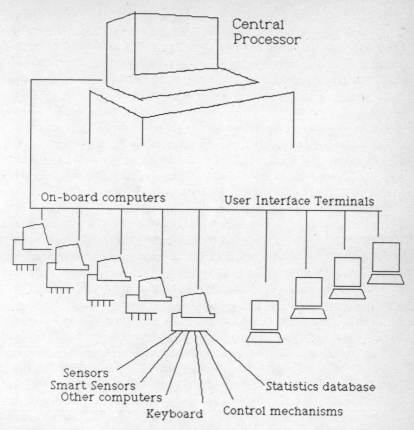

Figure 4.7 A possible physical arrangement of the IKBS.

However, the software techniques still need to be developed. This work is being done in universities, but their current level of support means that progress will be slow. Further miniaturisation of hardware could help, because less efficient software could be accommodated on faster processors. However, this does not guarantee that the software will be adequately tested and work as expected.

Parts of the IKBS described above already exist. The design ensures that the system could be implemented in several easy stages. The feasibility horizon is not far away.

Concluding remarks

The IKBS described above is intended to suggest a unification of the existing activities within process control. The emphasis has been on symbolic techniques, because we wanted to show where these would be useful. This is not intended to preclude the use of mathematical techniques where they are useful. Indeed, the best kind of system would be one which could use both, so that mathematical techniques are used where precise data are available, and symbolic computation used where that is the most appropriate. Special-purpose processor architecture would ensure that the computation tasks are performed in the most time-efficient manner.

Many people are frightened by the prospect of humans' losing employment by the introduction of advanced automation. People are frightened, too, by the risks involved in managing complex industrial plant, as at Three Mile Island, Flixborough, Bhopal, Seveso and now Chernobyl. The ideas expressed above are intended to increase safety and efficiency in the operation of complex plant. Only some of the jobs in a plant can be replaced by computers, because the machines are making new jobs for themselves, by taking on tasks that humans could never do well, because of their tedium or magnitude. There are things that humans can do bettter than computers, because of our inherent flexibility and accordingly we have emphasised the role of training so that workers are given the opportunity to learn from the IKBS, en-skilling rather than de-skilling their jobs.

The intelligent machines outlined above represent the future of automation in industrial control. Parts of what have been described have already been implemented and are being used routinely in industry now. Other parts are the subject of research in universities. The architecture outlined above has been deliberately designed so that it can be introduced piecemeal, a little bit at a time. Industry's caution likes to apply the 'salami approach' to the introduction of change.

However, what has been described is not far from possibility. The next generation of hardware and software could see it happen. Techniques in the USA and Japan could bring these ideas to fulfilment in one or two years. If this talk were presented at the American or Japanese Association for the Advancement of Science, the Europeans would be quaking in their boots. At the British Association, they would be dismissed as the ambitious fantasies of a young dreamer. Isambard Kingdom Brunel would not be so daunted were he alive today.

Acknowledgements

The author gratefully acknowledges the co-operation of her colleagues in the Knowledge Engineering Applications Group of the Department of Electrical and Electronic Engineering at Queen Mary College, many of whom are working to bring about some of the ideas expressed in this paper.

References

Hart, P. E., Duda, R. O. and Einaudi, M. T. (1978), 'A Computer-based Consultation System for Mineral Exploration', Technical Report, SRI International, May.

Koukoulis, C. G. (1986), 'The Application of Knowledge Based Techniques to Industrial Maintenance Problems', PhD thesis, Queen Mary College, University of London, February.

Kuipers, B. (1985), 'The Limits of Qualitative Simulation', 9th International Joint Conference on Artificial Intelligence, Los Angeles, August.

Mamdani, E. H. (1974), 'Application of Fuzzy Algorithms for the Control of a Simple Dynamic Plant', *Proc. IEE*, **121**, 12, pp. 1585–8.

Minsky, M. (1975). 'A Framework for Representing Knowledge' in P. Winston, ed., *The Psychology of Computer Vision*, New York: McGraw-Hill.

Shortliffe, E. H. (1976), *Computer-based Medical Consultations: MYCIN*, New York: Elsevier.

5 Expert systems and evidential reasoning

*James Baldwin**

Introduction

An expert system is a computer program which emulates a human expert in some restricted domain of application from the point of view of solving problems. Such problems are taking decisions under uncertainty, planning and giving advice in such areas as medical diagnosis, engineering fault finding, vision and speech recognition, robotics, manufacturing and banking. People can be given advice by an expert system in many areas, including what rights they have, what investments they should make, where to find the appropriate information, and so on.

An expert system consists of two parts. One part is a knowledge-base consisting of that knowledge of the domain of application used by the expert in his performance in answering questions about the area of his expertise. A second part is an inference engine which controls how queries are answered when the user asks questions. The inference engine should be able to perform some form of evidential reasoning resembling the way in which a human expert would use his knowledge and observations to draw conclusions.

Human experts use heuristics, rules of thumb whose truth cannot be guaranteed but, never the less, work on most occasions. They learn from experience, quickly reject unpromising lines of argument, create explanations for surprising results and can use concepts which cannot be defined by specifying a set of necessary and sufficient conditions.

An expert system must be able to do similar tasks if it is to emulate the human expert. How can this be achieved? This paper will discuss some of these issues and in particular describe a support logic programming system called SLOP (Baldwin 1986; 1987; Baldwin and Monk 1985) which will run Prolog programs but also allow inferences to be made based on heuristics and uncertain data. In

*Director of Information Technology Research Centre, University of Bristol

SLOP evidence is obtained from different viewpoints via the knowledge-base to support a given conclusion. Evidence can be not only incomplete but also conflicting. The inference rules of SLOP will resolve any conflicts and determine a support for the conclusion. It is an ideal language for developing expert-system shells and modelling problems in the real world, taking into account the difficulty of obtaining precise information and being able to define complex concepts precisely.

Intelligent behaviour is not simply about weighing up various evidences to arrive at a conclusion. It is characterised by a sophisticated self-adaptive ability, a means of creating generalisations from specific instances and other forms of learning. Present-day expert systems are rudimentary in this respect for their knowledge acquisition relying more on the complete knowledge of the human expert being transferred to the computer. This transfer is difficult and some way of automating this in addition to the expert system learning for itself will be required in the future. A promising approach for this is the application of Kelly's Personal Construct Theory to knowledge acquisition (Shaw 1981). One has to know a lot before one can learn for oneself. Large knowledge-bases require some form of parallel processing to get at the information required at the right time. The brain, with its slow biological components, is much quicker than the serial computer, with its very fast electronic components, at certain tasks involving large knowledge-bases. Learning requires large amounts of knowledge. It might be said that the computer is fast but slow in thinking while the brain is slow but fast in thinking. It is doubtful if present-day computer architectures can provide the speed of response necessary to provide any thing other than the most elementary form of learning systems. Machine learning is in its infancy but research is progressing in this area (Michalski *et al*. 1983).

The theory of search is a fundamental study in artificial intelligence. The search for solutions to a given problem includes the search for an appropriate method and an appropriate solution path. One idea common in AI is that a programming language should be used to specify the problem at hand. The system can then be queried to provide answers to specific questions. For example, the specification may be a list of pairs of people who are married to each other. We may be interested to know if Mary is married to any one. This would be asked as a query and the system would provide its own method of deducing the answer. First-order logic can be used to write the specification and a general theorem prover used to provide the answer to a question expressed in first-order logic. The query above would be asked by asking the system to prove the proposition that there exists a person such that Mary is married to that person. In proving this to be a theorem the system would extract the information of who that person is. The general theorem prover would use a search strategy to prove the theorem. This search strategy can be made more efficient by using heuristics to guide the search. Even then the approach is too inefficient for logic to be used in this way as a programming language. If certain constraints are placed on the language of first-order logic then efficient proof procedures can be used and one example of such a language is Prolog. The support logic programming language SLOP is also an example of this but allows an uncertainty to be associated with the statements in the knowledge base.

The jug problem and expert systems

Consider the problem of filling a seven-gallon jug with four gallons of water when a five-gallon jug is available also for use. Each jug can be filled with water or emptied and water can be transferred from one jug to another. This is a well-known problem and has been discussed in relation to expert systems by Kowalski and Sergot (1984). We could solve the problem using a search strategy to find the solution. One would have to avoid looping, that is, arriving at a same position as previously after several operations. Alternatively one can use the following rules:

1. Whenever the big container is empty, fill it.
2. Whenever the small container is full, empty it.
3. In all other cases, transfer as much water as possible from the large container to the small one.

A record is kept of how much water is in each container and the process stops when the required amount is in the seven-gallon jug.

These rules could be thought of as rules coming from an expert. They are not at all obvious and will solve any jug problem of this form. In actual fact the rules are both sound and complete in that any solution generated will be correct and any problem that can be solved will be solved with these rules. The problem is of course very simple. In general for more complex situations it will not be possible to provide rules which will guarantee the correct solution each time. The rules will more often be heuristics.

The above system can be validated but when we use heuristics, as is generally true with expert systems, an important question is how we can validate such systems. It might be thought that some form of refutation should be used as in a Popperian approach to scientific method (Popper 1959). In other words we should test the performance of the system under the most stringent conditions we can think of. This would, of course, work if we did not accept that the rules of the expert system are heuristics and can therefore be inappropriate on some occasions. What criteria should we use to assess the importance of a refutation when found? This is an open question which we will leave the reader to think about.

Support logic programming and expert systems

If we know that we are using heuristics then we should give some indication of our support on the general use of the rule. Consider, for example, the rule

IF a man is tall THEN he wears large shoes

No one would wish to say that this rule is always applicable but most people would probably agree that it is a good heuristic. In what sense should we use it and how good a heuristic is it? The support logic programming system allows a pair of supports

[nec_sup, pos_sup]

to be associated with this rule. Each support is a number in the range [0, 1] with the further constraint that

$$nec\_sup + pos\_sup \leq 1$$

The nec_sup is a measure of the support of the consequent given the antecedent of the rule while $(1 - pos\_sup)$ is a measure of the necessary support for the negation of the consequent given the antecedent of the rule. Thus we can speak of the pos_sup as representing the possible support of the consequent given the antecedent of the rule.

As a special case the support pairs can be thought of as a probability interval. In the above example, this would correspond to saying that the probability of the consequent being true given that the antecedent is true lies between nec_sup and pos_sup. Similarly, the probability that the consequent is false given the antecedent is true lies between $(1 - \text{pos\_sup})$ and $(1 - \text{nec\_sup})$. This law of negation is more complicated than the point value case.

It should be emphasised that a piece of evidence can support a given conclusion to a degree less than 1 but give no support for the negation of the conclusion. For example, having a sore throat gives some, if only a small, support for the person having flu but this system gives no support for the person not having flu.

We need a rule for determining the support for a person wearing large shoes if there is some support for the person being tall. This support would be given in the form of a support pair as above. This rule is provided by the support logic theory as given by Baldwin (1986; 1987). An interesting case arises if we know that a person is well above average height. Knowing this must give some support for that person being tall. In other words, there is some match between the concepts of being tall and being well above average height. This is called 'semantic unification' in the support logic programming system. SLOP actually calculates the support pair for tall given above average height and this support pair is associated with the hidden rule

a person is tall IF that person has height well above average

The rule is hidden in the sense that the system injects this rule temporarily into the knowledge-base prior to answering the query.

The support pair associated with this rule is determined using the definitions of 'tall' and 'well above average' in the knowledge-base expressed as fuzzy sets on the height space associated with people. The theories of fuzzy sets and possibility theory have been developed by Zadeh (1978). Fuzzy sets can also be defined by means of recursive rules within the support logic programming system. The recursive rules for defining the concept of tall person basically states that if a little height is taken from a tall person there is strong support for the person still being tall and no support against this. The interpretation of 'strong support' is a number close to 1 but not equal to 1, otherwise one obtains the paradox that all persons are tall. This is not the only rule required but the other rules are similar in nature. A possibility and necessity measure associated with fuzzy set theory is used to determine the support pair.

The following are some rules expressed in the support logic programming system:

guilty(william,crime) : [1/4,5/6]

states that there is a necessary support of 1/4 that William is guilty of the crime and a necessary support of $(1 - 5/6) = 1/6$ that he is not. The determination of the supports may have come from a jury of twelve who are able to vote 'guilty', 'not guilty' or 'abstain'. In this case three jurors voted 'guilty', two jurors voted 'not guilty' and seven abstained.

is_heavy(X) :- is_very_heavy(X) : [1,1]

says that anything (X is a variable that can be instantiated to any object) that is very heavy is necessarily heavy. The symbol :- can be read as 'IF'. So that the statement reads 'X is heavy IF X is very heavy'. The support pair [1,1] corresponds to absolute truth.

married(X,Y) :- married(X,Z), not $Z = Y$: [0,0].

says that no one can be married to more than one person. The support pair [0,0]] corresponds to absolute false. This rule states that if X is married to Z and Y is different from Z then there cannot be any support for X being married to Y.

is_very_heavy(X) :- is_heavy(X) : [0,1].

says that it is totally uncertain whether X is very heavy or not when given that X is heavy. The support pair [0,1] corresponds to totally uncertain, since it corresponds to zero support for and zero support against.

Consider the support logic program:

```
wears_large_shoes(X) :- is_tall(X) : [0.7,1].
is_tall(X) :- is_heavy(X), not is_fat(X) : [0.9,1].
is_tall(X) :- has_height(X,H), tall(H).
tall(70) : [0.8,0.9].
is_heavy(john) : [0.9,1].
is_fat(john) : [0,0.1].
has_height(john,70).
```

We can now ask the query 'does John wear large shoes?' which is expressed as

?- wears_large_shoes(john).

The support logic programming system returns the answer:

wears large shoes(john) : [0.6621, 1].

It determines this in the following manner. In order to prove wear_large_shoes(john), it uses the first statement above and concludes it must first prove is_tall(john) which it does with the associated support pair [0.9558, 1]. This is then combined with the support pair [0.7,1] using the implication rule to conclude the answer given. The rules for SLOP are given in the next section. No justification will be given in this paper for these rules but this can be found in Baldwin (1986; 1987).

The proposition is_tall(john) can be proved in two ways. Firstly it can be proved using the third, seventh and fourth statements in a similar manner to the above calculation to give a support pair [0.8,1] to is_tall(john). Secondly it can be proved by using the second, fifth and sixth statements to give the support pair [0.729,1] to is_tall(john). For this it is necessary to determine a support pair for the conjunction is_heavy(john), not is_fat(john) and this determined using the product rule for conjunction after calculating the support for not is_fat(john) using the negation rule.

We now have two support pairs for the statement is_tall(john) which arise from independent viewpoints. These are combined into a final support using the rule of combination given below. This takes into account any conflict between the two supports. For example, any support given to is_tall(john) AND not is_tall(john) determined by the product rule is shared among the other possible statements in the same proportion as their original supports so that the modified support for is_tall(john) AND not is_tall(john) is zero.

SLOP rules

We can now give the rules for support logic programming calculus for determining the support pair for a given proof path and also for combining the support pairs of different proof paths to give an overall support. We will use the multiplication model in stating these rules but the rules can be modified to allow for any of the other models discussed above. The complete logic programming system allows for any of the models to be used.

IF

fact1(X) : [f1n,f1p].
fact2(X) : [f2n,f2p].
fact3(X) : [f3na,f3pa].
rule(X) :- fact1(X) : [rn,rp].

prob_rule(X) :- fact1(X) : [pn,pp].
prob_rule(X) :- NOT fact1(X) : [npn,npp].

THEN

1. Conjunction
fact1(X),fact2(X) : [cn,cp]
where
cn = f1n·f2n ; cp = f1p·f2p

2. Disjunction
fact1(X);fact2(X) : [dn,dp]
where
dn = f1n + f2n − f1n·f2n ; dp = f1p + f2p − f1p·f2p

3. Negation
NOT fact1(X) : [nn,np]
where
nn = 1 − f1p ; np = 1 − f1n

4. Conditional
rule(X) : [icn,icp]
where
icn = rn·f1n ; icp = 1 − (1 − rp)·f1n

5. Probability Rule
pro_rule(X) : [prn,prp]
where
prn = pn·f1n + (1−f1n)·npn ; 1 − ((1−f1p)·(1−npp) +(1−pp)·f1n)

6. Same conclusion
fact3(X) : [scn,scp]
where
conflict = − f3na·(1 − f3pb) + f3nb·(1 − f3pa)
csn = (f3na+f3nb−f3na·f3nb−conflict)/(1−conflict)
scp = (f3pa·f3pb)/(1−conflict)

Evidence theory paradoxes and SLOP and bundles

It has been argued (Salmon 1983) that two pieces of evidence, taken separately, can both confirm quite strongly a given hypothesis whilst the conjunction of these pieces of evidence reduces the confirmation of it. To take one of his examples, consider the chess-playing competition in which players are 'local' or 'out-of-towners' and 'junior' or

	h local player			g out-of-towner	
junior j	m	w	w	m	m
senior s	m	m		w	w	w

Figure 5.1

'senior'. Each player is male (m) or female (w) and they are distributed as given in Figure 5.1. Let f be the hypothesis that a male player will win. We assume that each player is equally likely to win and this is background information e. Let $c(.|.)$ be a conditional confirmation function;
then

$c(f|e) = 1/2$

while

$c(f|e,h) = 3/5$ and $c(f|e,j) = 3/5$

but

$c(f|e,h,j) = 1/3$

Thus

$c(f|e,h) - c(f|e) = +1/10$
$c(f|e,j) - c(f|e) = +1/10$
$c(f|e,h,j) - c(f|e) = -1/6$

showing that the pieces of evidence, h and j, taken separately both confirm f but the conjunction of the evidences reduces the confirmation for f.

We can avoid this paradox by using support pairs as given below. When only one piece of evidence is used it is important to realise that other information could have been obtained. If this other information is not collected, the fact that it could have been collected must be taken into account.

Given that the winner is a local player, then the winner will be male with a probability = 1/3 if the winner is a junior and a male with a probability = 1 if the winner is a senior. Therefore

f :- h : [1/3,1].

Similarly

f :- j : [1/3,1].

Suppose we also know

h : [1,1].
j:[1,1].

Then

$\quad$ f : $[1/3,1]$

and

$\quad$ f : $[1/3,1]$

using the two proof paths for f and we must combine these solutions by intersecting the two intervals to obtain

$\quad$ f : $[1/3,1]$

which is consistent with $\Pr(f|h,j) = 1/3$ and $\Pr(\text{NOT } f|h,j) = 2/3$.

We can exploit this use of support pairs to allow bundles of statements in the support logic programming language. A bundle of statements is a collection of statements expressing different forms of the same rule. Different forms are required in practice to allow for incomplete information on some of the conjuncts of the conjunctive part of the rule. For example, consider the bundle

$\quad$ good_student(X,C) :- <- intelligent(X),
$\qquad\qquad\qquad\qquad\qquad$ hard_working(X),
$\qquad\qquad\qquad\qquad\qquad$ well_motivated(X,C) : $[0.7,0.8]$
$\qquad\qquad\qquad\qquad\qquad$ intelligent(X),
$\qquad\qquad\qquad\qquad\qquad$ well_motivated(X,C) : $[0.6,0.8]$.

If we know for sure that John is intelligent, hard working and well motivated to computer science then we would use the first rule to conclude with some support pair that John would be a good student on a computer science course. On the other hand if we were totally unsure of whether or not John is hard working, we would use the second rule to determine the support pair. For intermediate cases when we know to some extent each of the three factors, it is not obvious which rule should be used. SLOP determines a support pair using each of the rules in the bundle and takes the intersection of all the resulting support pair intervals. Any point in the solution support pair interval must be a point in each of the individual support pair intervals arising from use of the rules. This is so since all the rules in the bundle are assumed consistent. In this example the support pair for the second rule is determined by considering the two cases hard_working and not hard_working separately and taking the union of the support pairs for each case.

Knowledge representation and inference

How can we best store information in the computer and what methods should we use to make deductions, inductions and abductions from it? In this paper we have suggested that logic can provide a way of representation and deduction. Theories of belief, knowledge, rationality, and so on, are required in the study of AI. One should not at this time draw any definite conclusions on what the best form of representation, and hence deduction, is.

An alternative form of knowledge representation is that of conceptual structures as described in Sowa (1984). A language, CRIL, based on this is described in Baldwin and Crabtree (1986) and examples of its use for inference given.

A conceptual graph is a directed graph with two sorts of node, concept nodes and relation nodes. The theory brings together many topics from the semantic net approach of AI, linguistics, and first-order, modal and higher-order logics. A type lattice for the concepts provides information for an inheritance theory so that types are allowed to share properties from supertypes. Operations exist to join graphs, restrict and generalise concepts, simplify graphs and project graphs onto graphs. This gives a mathematical framework for representing AI theories and CRIL can be used to express such theories in a computer.

A sentence can be represented by a conceptual graph and a sentence with the same meaning but different syntax is represented by the same or an equivalent graph. Thus semantics rather than syntax dominate the theory. Basic graph operations can generate a set of meaningful graphs from a base set and this is equivalent to the approach of Schank (1982).

A learning theory from examples and counter-examples can be derived using conceptual graphs and their matching operations. Support pairs are generated expressing how well an object represented as a conceptual graph can be matched against the example set and against the counter example set. These are combined into a final support pair giving the support for the object representing this concept. The CRIL language has no intrinsic control strategy for answering queries and is an ideal language for implementation using a parallel computing architecture. Much of this work is in its infancy but gives a framework for knowledge representation and inference of a more general character than presently found in AI.

Conclusions

Several aspects of AI research have been discussed in this chapter. Particular emphasis has been placed on support logic programming,

SLOP, as a language most suitable for the development of expert-system shells. Uncertainty and incompleteness of information must be dealt with adequately if the technology of expert systems is to be useful for helping with the decision-making tasks associated with problems in the real world. These problems are difficult because of the incompleteness of information relevant for their solution.

References

Baldwin, J. F. (1986), 'Support Logic Programming' in A. Jones, A. Kaufmann and H. Zimmermann, eds, *Fuzzy Sets Theory and Applications*, D. Reidal.

Baldwin, J. F. (1987), 'Evidential Support Logic Programming', to appear in *Fuzzy Sets and Systems*.

Baldwin, J. F. and Crabtree, B. (1986), 'CRIL—A Concept Relational Inference Language' in Negoita and Prade, eds, *Fuzzy Logics in Knowledge Engineering*, Verlag TUV.

Baldwin, J. F. and Monk, R. (1985), 'Manual for SLOP', Internal Report, Information Technology Research Centre, University of Bristol.

Kowalski, R. A. and Sergot, M. J. (1984), 'Micro-Prolog for Problem Solving' in K. L. Clark and F. G. McCabe, eds, *Micro-Prolog*, Englewood Cliffs, NJ: Prentice-Hall.

Michalski, R. S., Carbonnell, J. G. and Mitchell, T. M. (1983), *Machine Learning*, Tioga.

Popper, K. (1959), *The Logic of Scientific Discovery*, New York: Basic Books.

Salmon, W. C. (1983), 'Confirmation and Relevance' in P. Achinstein, ed., *The Concept of Evidence*, Oxford: Oxford University Press.

Schank, R. C. (1982), *Dynamic Memory*, Cambridge: Cambridge University press.

Shaw, L. G. M. (1981), *Recent Advances in Personal Construct Theory*, Academic Press.

Sowa, J. F. (1984), *Conceptual Structures*, Adison Wesley.

Zadeh, L. A. (1978), 'Fuzzy Sets as a Basis for a Theory of Possibility', *Fuzzy Sets and Systems*, **1**, pp. 3–28.

6 Intelligence and the man-machine interface

Terry Walton

This chapter aims to show how the simple, familiar everyday telephone system has recently been developing and how these developments are now about to become apparent to the end-user. The secret of this development lies in the introduction of microelectronics, and particularly computer processing power, into the telephone network infrastructure. The new intelligent network that is gradually emerging is opening up exciting possibilities for both business and residential customers.

The story begins with that famous sentence from Alexander Graham Bell: 'Come here Watson, I want you.' These words, spoken in 1876, made up the first telephone conversation. Since that historic moment, the telephone has developed to become one of the most common and indispensible machines in our lives. In the UK alone, virtually every business and nearly 80 per cent of all households now have telephones, and over 24 billion telephone calls are made every year.

However, despite the remarkable spread of the telephone network, the basic function of the telephone has changed little since those early days. It is still used primarily to enable a degraded form of speech, cut down from a 16,000 Hz range to a reasonably intelligible 3,500 Hz, to be transmitted between two remote points. Despite the growth in data communications, it is worth observing that at present 'data' communications succeeds in spite of, rather than because of the telephone network.

In its simplest form, a telephone network comprises telephones connected to a local exchange by a pair of wires, called the local loop. Exchanges are grouped in clusters with a trunk exchange connected to each of its local groups by junction cables, while the trunk exchange itself is connected to other trunk exchanges by trunk cables. The fundamental components of this system are the switches and the

*Head of Network Information Services. Marketing, British Telecom

transmission links, the local ends, the junction and trunk cables. It is useful to study the way these have developed over the years.

Transmission systems

The first telephone service in the UK began some three years after Bell had first demonstrated his invention and was very much a local service with isolated communities growing up in different major centres. It took until 1898 to marshal the technology and finance to bring about the first long-distance link. This depended upon the simple expedient of using big, thick, low resistance copper cables to ensure that the signal reached the far end with sufficient power to be intelligible. It was not until 1916, twelve years after the invention of thermionic valves, that amplifier circuits or repeaters were incorporated into the network to enable smaller-guage cable to be used and greater distances to be achieved.

A further nineteen years elapsed before technology achieved the breakthrough of sending more than one conversation down a pair of wires. Within three years this technology had been refined and with the use of coaxial cables the modest three channels that had first been achieved was increased to forty. From then on there was a steady advance, accelerated by wartime advances in communication techniques, so that today's systems achieve as many as 2,000 conversations down a single coaxial cable.

Despite advances in the use of microwaves, and even the launch of Telstar, the most significant breakthrough occurred in 1964 when digital transmission was launched. The conversion of the analogue speech waveform into a train of binary digits was justified at the time purely on the grounds of lower equipment costs and improved quality in transmission. With hindsight, it can be seen that this was a fundamental step on the road to a revolution in communications.

Pulse code modulation (PCM) systems developed quickly from 1964 onwards, making use of the rapid advances in electronics from single-component through to large-scale integrated circuits, but the transmission medium remains coaxial cable. New, more efficient transmission systems were researched and a two-horse race developed between waveguides and optical fibre. The outcome is history.

Yet the trend towards greater transmission capacity continues. Commercial optical fibre systems are now carrying signals at 560 megabits per second, equivalent to 8,000 speech channels, and a recent development has doubled the transmission capacity of all fibres at a stroke by achieving two-way transmission in the same fibre. In the future, the use of different colours of light signal promises further multiplication of the capacity of the fibres now being installed.

Switching

The development of switching systems is in marked contrast with the steady progress in the transmission field. The first telephone service in the UK started out with manual cross-connection by operators to effect the 'switch'. In 1889, Alvin B. Strowger, a Kansas City undertaker, found he was losing business because the wife of his chief competitor was operating the Kansas City switchboard and was passing all calls from grieving parties straight to her husband. Taking time off from packing mortal remains, Strowger developed a simple electromagnetic relay set to replace the human operator, particularly his competitor's wife, and retain his business. Unfortunately, the history books do not record whether Strowger continued in his original profession!

The UK did not adopt the Strowger switch as rapidly as it did Bell's invention, and it took twenty-three years before the first Strowger switch was installed in Epsom in 1912. Strowger would surely have been amazed to find that about 100 years after his invention, he could walk into a British Telecom exchange and see equipment similar to his original design still whirring and clicking away. Over the years other forms of electromechanical switch have been developed but the Post Office maintained faith in Strowger, although the early 1960s saw signs of attempts to harness electronics into the switching function.

In 1962 an experimental electronic exchange was installed in Highgate Wood, London, but the story goes that as the exchange powered up, all the lights in the locality went out and the temperature in the exchange rose rapidly until the exchange was switched off. Nevertheless many valuable lessons were learnt. The experience clearly caused some radical rethinking because it was not until 1970 that the first alternative to Strowger switching started to appear in the Post Office's exchanges in the form of an alternative electromechanical system, the Crossbar exchange, and a quasi-electronic exchange, the TXE2. These first electronic exchanges were really little more than analogues of the old electromechanical switches, using electronic control to cross-connect physical pathways between two lines. The facilities provided for the customer remained exactly the same.

By the early 1970s, the success of PCM in transmission was pointing the way forward for switching and the search was under way for a switching system that could handle the PCM signals directly rather than reconvert them to analogue signals. The culmination of this quest was the arrival of the System X switch, first shown working in Geneva in 1979 and then put into service in 1980—the world's first truly digital exchange system. Since 1980, British Telecom has been installing digital exchanges at the heart of the network so that now virtually all the main trunk network is fully digital in both transmission and switching.

To most customers, this has so far been barely perceptible, although one of the principle benefits of digital transmission and switching, namely the elimination of noise on the line, has not gone unnoticed. We now get more trouble on our local networks and local junction transmission, although this too is being rapidly replaced. By the early 1990s the end of Strowger switches will be in sight, but not before clocking up 100 years of service—not bad for an undertaker.

Intelligent telephony

So, today digital technology is present in both transmission and switching fields. Yet they could be described as what in effect amounts to a better mousetrap: cheaper, clearer, more reliable, and noise-free telephony. The added dimension enabling the theme of 'living with intelligent machines' to be explored in the context of telephony is provided by looking into the world of computing where, in the space of twenty years, advances in technology have created and then repeatedly changed the face of computing and control.

In fairness to Highate Wood, the technology of the day was inadequate to meet the system requirements for an electronic switch cost-effectively. By the end of the 1970s, however the development of System X had run in parallel with developments in processing and storage technology to make the whole concept feasible and economic. The real bonus has been that the reduction of speech to digital streams coupled with the inclusion of digital processing capability within the switch, has turned electronic switching into a data-processing activity in which it becomes possible to conceive and implement new processes which do unusual things to the data (your voice) before they reach their final destination. As British Telecom begins to replace worn out electromechanical local exchanges with modern electronic switches, the possibilities will begin to reveal themselves to the user, at home and at work, in the form of new exchange services and new applications over the network.

Take the idea of the telephone exchange as a data-processing system and consider what it means in terms of the processes it is expected to perform. The telephone call consists of four phases. In the first phase, the caller must tell the exchange what is required, for example, connect to 246 8091. This is the 'signalling' phase. The exchange then switches the call, arranging for a pair of wires to be connected to some distant pair of wires. This is the switching phase. Once the switch has been effected, and the call has been answered, the communication phase is entered. The last phase occurs when one of the telephones is put down, sending a final signal to the exchange that the call is over.

In the new electronic system, the telephone line is now connected to a small computer called a line card, which constantly checks, waiting for commands. These can be sent in two different forms. One is the familiar click-clicking of the rotary dial, the other is a modern, fast and flexible tone signalling system called multi-frequency (MF) or touchtone. In the old Strowger system, the pulses generated by the telephone dial actually cause relays to operate so that the whole system responds directly to the turn of the dial. Whilst the call is in progress, a clockwork meter ticks away steadily, adding on call units for later charging. Not so with System X. Now the exchange waits until the signalling has been completed and then starts to process the instruction.

To continue with the call analogy, the switch now sends a message to the line card connected to the called party line and tells it to start ringing the phone and waits to hear that the phone has been answered. Once the two parties are connected, the communications phase is entered, during which the line card detects the noise made on the line and converts this into a 64-kilobits-per-second data stream which is transferred across to the called party's line card where it is reconverted to an analogue signal to send to the distant telephone. A similar data-conversion and transfer operation takes place in the opposite direction. The line card recognises when a phone has been replaced (because the line current ceases) and completes the call by making a data record of the call so that a charge can be made.

That is simple telephony but now it is possible to think about doing more complex processes. This is because the first phase of a call no longer results in the immediate direct physical response of setting relays in motion but is instead a set of instructions to an intelligent machine that can then be processed. So a sequence of numbers can be defined that result in an action other than a call set-up process. Unfortunately, existing dial telephones, and their modern push-button counterparts, can only send strings of from one to ten pulses and it is difficult to devise suitable control sequences for other functions which use numbers only.

Benefits of System X

The new exchanges will happily accept ordinary dial pulses as it would be impractical to change all telephones over immediately after an exchange has been replaced. But to enjoy the real benefits of the new exchanges, new telephones are required that have a greater repertoire of signals. System X has been designed to operate with the multi-frequency tone signalling system in which each character of the full 16 character set (0–9, *, #, A,B,C and D), is represented by a pair of tones, one from a set of four low frequency tones and one from a set of high frequency tones. In fact, telephones will not use the A,B,C,D digits but the extra * and # are vital to the creation of the command sequences to tell the exchange what you want it to do.

Here are some examples of things which the exchange can be made to do. Firstly, suppose the user is going out for the evening but is expecting an important telephone call. Of course it is possible to use an answering machine but perhaps it is too important even for that. A few keystrokes on the phone instruct the exchange to divert calls, at which point the exchange 'asks' to which number the calls are to be diverted—it holds a selection of words in a digital store, and can use them to speak back to the user. After hearing the voice prompt, the user can key in the number and the exchange will confirm that calls will now be diverted to that number. The exchange stores the number in its memory and will send all calls on to the specified alternative. When the user returns home the diversion can be cancelled by calling the exchange and sending the 'divert off' command sequence.

Suppose on the next call, the user is speaking to someone and both realise that there is a need to discuss a vital issue with a colleague—perhaps making arrangements for a meeting. On System X, it is possible to break off in mid-conversation without losing the distant end and tell the exchange that a second party is wanted on the line. The exchange then sets up the second call and when that has been established, the two conversations are added together digitally. The result is a quite natural sounding three-way conversation.

System X can also help when an incoming call is received whilst a call is already in progress. Instead of giving the engaged signal, the exchange can send a discreet signal to the called party to indicate that another call is waiting. It is then possible temporarily to switch over the the new call and return to the original call at a later stage.

These are the three most useful facilities available on System X though there are many more, such as 'automatic alarm calls', a much cheaper alternative to the operator service; and advice of call cost, where the phone rings immediately after a call has been completed and a pleasant voice announces the call cost and duration.

The exchange can also memorise a list of frequently called numbers which can then be summoned by a couple of keystrokes rather than a long sequence. Of course many modern phones store numbers but with many extensions it is perhaps easier to have numbers stored in one place.

Some facilities can only be used on calls to numbers on other System X exchanges, such as 'ring back when free', where the network will keep trying an engaged number and call back when the number is free.

The list goes on with the possibility of becoming ever more exotic. The beauty of the system is that more can be added by making program changes; there is a continuous process of program development in which new facilities are constantly being added to the system as they are thought up. For example, British Telecom already operates a service called Voicebank that acts very much like an answering and recording machine but with more advanced features. One disadvantage of Voicebank is that a separate Voicebank telephone number is needed which callers must know in order to leave a message. As System X is developed, however, the storage could be integrated into the network so that calls may be answered automatically if required. Another group of exchange facilities makes use of the fact that the phone line is actually very rarely used for making calls. In fact an average domestic telephone line is actually in use for less than 2 per cent of the time. This idle capacity could be put to good use by attaching other equipment in the home which can help to run the house—perhaps a burglar and fire alarm system and an attachment for reading the gas and electricity meters.

Future applications

The facilities outlined so far are provided directly by the intelligence at the heart of the network. However, the technology which has allowed creation of the digital network has also been exploited in stand-alone systems that can be added to the existing network and gradually integrated into the system as it becomes more widespread.

In years to come, it will become increasingly commonplace for people to use the telephone network to make transactions which are not conversations. There is an almost symbiotic relationship between the development of the new applications and the introduction of System X, as many of the new facilities will depend upon the MF signalling capability of the telephones which users will have. A key benefit of the MF signalling system is that the tones use frequencies which are part of the speech band which forms the standard telephone channel, so they can be transmitted across the network without corruption. It is quite possible to use the MF signals to operate equipment remotely, even across continents.

Many countries have already adopted MF4 as their standard exchange signalling system and in those countries it is already possible to find examples of applications which will shortly become available here. Some interesting uses for the MF/voice response technology include home banking; ordering goods from catalogues, by keying in item codes and credit card numbers; or even ordering goods advertised on television, using the power of an automatic system to process the flood of calls that can occur when people respond directly to a TV advert.

Of course, it is going to be a long time before everyone has an MF telephone but interactive services will be available in the near future as already there are systems that respond directly to the human voice. Voice recognition has been developing slowly and we are still many years away from systems that will respond to a large vocabulary of words spoken by a large number of people. This is particularly so for speech as heard at the end of a telephone line but compromises and trade-offs can be made so that by using a limited vocabulary, like 0–9 and yes and no, voice recognition can be made to work in a relatively speaker-independent way.

Alternatively, a wider vocabulary can be trained into the system for a limited number of users for more sophisticated applications. There is a great deal of overlap between interactive systems which use voice recognition and MF tones, which are, after all, only another kind of recognisable sound, and it is possible to envisage systems that use both facilities, offering options appropriate for the particular tasks. It might be that at some point in the distant future it will be possible to pick up a phone and say 'please get 246 8091'—which almost takes us back to where we started.

Another potential use of MF signalling is remote control of household apparatus. The meter-reading system described earlier is being developed to provide a sophisticated load-control facility primarily for the benefit of the Elecricity Boards who will be able selectively to switch off household appliances such as water heaters at critical loading times. This should benefit consumers because it will greatly reduce the need for standby capacity in the generating system, thereby bringing down costs. The system could be developed to give customers a remote control facility, too, for example, switching on water heating on return from holiday, or switching on lights to deter burglars, or perhaps even switching on the video recorder to record a program at short notice. All this could be achieved quite easily using a simple portable tone sender to send commands down the line.

The digital recording of voice and the ability to reconstruct message sequences is now being developed to provide an ever-increasing range of information and entertainment services, initially available by dialling particular telephone numbers, but ultimately incorporating interaction of MF signalling and voice recognition. British Telecom has already experimented with a talking railway timetable and a simple adventure game call 'Penny Green' that allows callers to explore a coastal hamlet in search of smuggler's treasure. Both these experiments used voice recognition.

The impact of the new network has so far been considered in terms of its impact on domestic customers who for the immediate future will continue to depend upon the simple pair of copper wires to carry calls to the exchange. It will be well into the next century before optical fibres start to appear in the residential local network. But for business customers, where the number of lines from one site to an exchange is great enough, it is already well worth converting the service from a mass of analogue copper pairs to a digital circuit either on coaxial cable or, in some instances now, on optical fibre. Once the digital link has been established into the customer's premises, a whole new range of possibilities opens up.

Data communications

Data communications has struggled over the years to try to squeeze digital signals down the telephone line. To do this, it has been necessary to convert data into an analogue waveform using a device called a modem so that the data can pass successfully across the network. How ironic that once into the network, the modem's analogue signal is immediately digitised into a 64-kilobits-per-second data stream only to be reconverted to analogue at the far end so that it can be turned into a digital output by the modem at the other end. And it is even more frustrating that the best data speeds possible are limited to only 9,600 bits per second. The extension of the digital path to the customer now means that data can exploit the full potential of the digital network at 64 kilobits per second or, by coupling a number of circuits together, achieve megabit transmission speeds.

Centrex

Centrex is a facility that is rapidly catching on in the USA, where the process of converting local switches to digital working is already under way. The idea behind Centrex is that the local exchange can play the part of the company's switchboard system rather than have an independent unit on company premises. For many years, companies have preferred to operate their own private switch (or PABX) partly because of the advanced facilities that could be made available to employees locally and also for quite real economic benefits. But the balance is now tipping in favour of the alternative solution in which a company rents a partition of the nearest local exchange that can not only provide all the sophisticated facilities required but can also be expanded and contracted to meet the company's changing needs. If the concept is taken further, a whole company network can be constructed from segments of the public network eliminating the inefficiencies of the current practice of building separate private networks which often lie idle for much of the day.

Smart building

Once a building is directly connected to the local exchange the kind of facilities mentioned earlier for energy management and security in the home can be extended out from the exchange to the office block.

The 'smart building' concept is particularly valuable in instances where the building has many different users. It means that the building is wired up from the onset with all the communications and management facilities required run off the local exchange. As tenants come and go, the facilities required can be simply switched on or off without any need for new switchboards, new wiring plans and reorganisations every time there is a change.

Audio conferencing and image transmission

The advent of high-speed digital communications into the work-place has made it possible to introduce a whole range of new applications, or significantly to enhance existing facilities. Audio conferencing is a typical example of a much needed facility which has been held back over the years because of the limitations of the old analogue network.

In the new digital era, conference calls between a large number of parties can be achieved by bringing the digital channels together and mixing them into a conference. This has been possible in the past only by working through a long and complicated setting-up procedure with the operator. Now it can be done automatically through the exchange. Moreover, by mixing the digital speech and text it will be possible to supplement the conference proceedings with images or documents. The 64-kilobits-per-second speed is ideal for document transmission, particularly for facsimile, where it becomes possible to transmit a good quality copy of a document in just four seconds instead of the minute or so required by existing machines on the analogue network.

Video image transmission

Facsimile demonstrates the fact that images as well as voice can be transmitted over the network, but what about a quality TV image? A broadcast-quality TV signal can be transformed into a digital stream, but the consequences are rather daunting at 140 megabits per second. By reducing the requirements, however, the demand on transmission can be brought down to manageable levels. First of all, movement can be eliminated and a still picture only sent. At full-quality full-screen size, this requires about six megabits to transmit. If the image is reduced in size to one-eighth of the total screen area and data-compression techniques are used, the image can be sent down the line in about 12 seconds. This is the basis of photovideotex, a new service which is being developed as an advanced viewdata service. At present its requirements for the 64-kilobits-per-second transmission limits its availability to business applications, but some potential uses, such as by estate agents and travel agents, could well lead to benefits for domestic customers in the near future.

The ability to digitise a picture and then freeze it in storage for onward transmission at 64 kilobits per second can also be used to prove a slow-scan TV facility, in which an image is updated at regular intervals, say every four seconds, so that any movement in a field of view can be detected. Such systems are already used extensively for on-site surveillance but, with 64-kilobits-per-second transmission, it now becomes possible to provide surveillance at remote sites. Other recent developments in processing the digital TV images are bringing forward the possibility of video conferencing, though for the forseeable future this will still require transmission speeds of two megabits per second and even at this speed the success of the technique depends upon techniques of data compression in which only the parts of the picture that have changed are transmitted. This is fine for an application such as conferencing, where small head or even just lip movements are taking place, but rapid movements, like standing up, overwhelm the system and the image breaks up dramatically.

The list of possible applications and facilities which the new intelligent network provides is, of course, much longer. This paper has dealt with the major ideas and those facilities which are destined to appear in the near future, rather than hypothesise about some distant technological wonderland. Many of the examples given here are already in service and developing rapidly:

- System X local exchanges are already installed and we now have ordinary domestic and business customers using the advanced exchange facilities.
- Digitally stored voice messages are now being used to provide a wide range of information and entertainment on the Premium Rate Services network.
- The London Integrated Digital Access pilot trial now has working connections at 64 kilobits to businesses in the London area, and optical fibres are now being run out to customer premises to meet requirements for high capacity voice and data transmission.

The shiny, new intelligent digital network is lying just beneath the grimy surface of old electromechanical switchgear. We are now at least scratching away at the surface to reveal the bright new system underneath. Over the next few years, the results of British Telecom's efforts should become apparent to everyone.

But before the benefits can be fully enjoyed, human habits will need to be developed. The new clever network can give us what is needed only if users learn how to control it. A great deal of effort has been made to ensure that the system is genuinely 'user friendly'. Now it is up to users to become 'system friendly'.

7 Turing's conception of intelligence
Andrew Hodges

Fifty years ago, on 28 August 1936, the young British mathematician Alan M. Turing (1912–1954) completed a paper with the obscure title 'On Computable Numbers, with an Application to the Entscheidungs problem'. It was a paper in mathematical logic, a subject which in the 1930s would have seemed as abstruse and as irrelevant to the practical world as could be imagined. Yet the concept of the *Turing machine*, introduced in this paper, is now recognised as the foundation of modern computer science.

Indeed Turing himself, in 1945, went on to plan in detail the development of an electronic digit computer and its applications. He was able to combine the ideas of his 1936 paper with the practical experience of electronic technology which he gained as Britain's chief cryptanalyst during the Second World War.

Turing's paper is also the first statement of the fundamental thesis of 'artificial intelligence': the principle that mental operations can be successfully modelled by a logical machine. This idea Turing also explored further after the war.

Turing confronts us with 'creative intelligence' in several ways. Firstly, the content of his work is all to do with the question of how minds work and what intelligence is. Secondly, we are faced with Turing's *own* creative intelligence, and with fascinating glimpses of the roots of his original ideas. But further, Turing presents an example of that British story: the great advances in research which are not matched by practical implementation. The very advanced ideas and experience that Turing offered in 1945 were not successfully exploited. In some ways his kind of intelligence was unable to complete the act of creation.

This chapter will try to describe a little on all these topics. It will survey the background to Turing's 1936 paper, and the idea of the Turing machine. It will explain why mathematical thought had come to the point of requiring an analysis of mental activity such as Turing

*Research Fellow, Mathematical Institute, University of Oxford.

was the first to provide, and will stress the wide range of influences, both intellectual and emotional, which contributed to Turing's ability to tackle the question. It will explain why the 1936 paper held not only this psychological analysis but also the essential idea of the computer, and survey the impact of Turing's thought on developments after 1945. It will draw on Turing's own lively and popular writing to illustrate his predictions about what he called 'intelligent machinery'.

It is now just fifty years since Alan Turing gave a new foundation to the discussion of 'intelligence' by presenting the mathematical model of the Turing machine. Turing did this in his paper [1] 'On Computable Numbers, with an Application to the Entscheidungsproblem', dated 28 August 1936. Turing was then a Cambridge research fellow of twenty-four and until then almost unknown. The paper presented a solution to an outstanding problem in mathematical logic, although it contained much more than this. I want to mark the anniversary of Turing's paper, but not from a technical standpoint. I wish to remark upon the breadth and variety of ideas that informed Turing's scientific inspiration, and the correspondingly wide implications of his ideas.

It may sound odd to speak of 'scientific inspiration' in connection with logic. But it ought to sound odd. What Turing did was very odd. He chose to look at logic as though it could lead to scientific information about the world. To understand this we need to examine Turing's early motivations.[2]

Turing had read mathematics at Cambridge and established himself as a mathematician, but he had gone there highly stimulated by the physics of Eddington and Einstein. He was also deeply concerned with understanding the nature of mind, the puzzle of its embodiment in the brain, and the classical problems of free will and determinism. His fascination with deterministic explanation was greatly sharpened by the death in 1930 of his school-friend Christopher Morcom, a young man who meant as much to him as anyone. He became deeply concerned by questions about the survival of the mind after death and, influenced by Eddington, he looked to quantum mechanics as a way to escape the old materialism of nineteenth-century physics. We should acknowledge an emotional component in the origins of Turing's scientific enquiry—certainly part of his creative intelligence.

Quantum theory was enjoying enormous success at that time. Turing was particularly impressed when Dirac's prediction of anti-

matter, a prediction which flowed mathematically from the fundamentals of quantum mechanics and relativity, was vindicated in 1932.
There was new scope for mathematical thought in physics, and he had
introduced himself to it very quickly. Mathematical physics was the
natural course for him to follow. It was therefore very odd that
Turing should have followed up the small and, professionally speaking, very marginal area of mathematical logic. But it seems that he
sensed that logic could hold a clue to the question which most deeply
concerned him—the nature of mind.

The logical problem which he tackled was the decision problem—the *Entscheidungsproblem*. The problem had been posed by
Hilbert, as part of a programme for making sense of the logical
foundations of mathematics. The problem is this: is there any definite
method which can be applied to a given mathematical assertion and
which will decide whether that is true? Superficially, this has nothing
whatever to do with problem of mind. But Turing saw a connection
because of the difficulty of defining what is meant by 'a definite
method'. It was a question which lay outside mathematics. In fact, it
was the difficulty of giving a satisfactory definition to this concept
that constituted the crux of the problem.

Turing seized upon the idea that a definite method was to be a
mechanical process, one that could be laid down in advance and
applied independently of human judgement or choice. Other people
had used these words 'mechanical' and 'machine', but it was Turing
who set out to make a precise definition of a logical machine—a
Turing machine—that could carry out a mechanical process acting on
symbols.

The Turing machine is now a standard construction in mathematics
and computer science and I shall not give details which are to be
found in textbooks.[3] Turing's original terms are interesting, however.
He thought of symbols inscribed on a tape marked off in squares. The
machine itself can have a finite number of 'configurations'—a term
which he could have taken from quantum mechanics. A 'table of
behaviour'—a more psychological term—defines exactly what the
machine will do in reading, writing, moving along the tape, and
changing to a new configuration. A Turing machine is allowed only a
very limited repertoire of possible behaviour—a sort of atomic theory
of logical operations, which are broken down into primitive con-
situents. Each different Turing machine—each different 'table of
behaviour'—corresponds to a different 'definite method'.

Once the Turing machine is adopted as a definition of 'definite method', the answer to Hilbert's question follows: there is no Turing machine that can solve all mathematical problems. In fact the Turing machine definition leads to an absolute of computability. Some numbers—indeed most numbers—cannot be computed. It was a very surprising discovery that such an absolute exists, the more so as it turns out to coincide with definitions arising from quite different approaches.

However, one must justify the claim that Turing machines, although built out of very primitive elements, are sufficiently all-encompassing to include anything one could possibly describe as a 'definite method'. This is an argument which is outside mathematics proper, and so much of Turing's paper is non-mathematical.

Turing had a general argument for this. He imagined a person applying such a method, and at every stage writing down a complete statement of what to do next in such a way that someone else could take over. He showed that such 'instruction notes' could be considered equivalent to the configurations of a Turing machine.

But he also proposed another, much more daring argument. In this, he did not require that the method being applied should be consciously described at every time. He just imagined the method being effected by a person who has a sequence of mental operations. He suggested that the person's mind could be considered as being in just one of a finite number of mental states, and that a 'definite method' could be regarded as a definite rule about what the person would do in each mental state. In this interpretation the mental states correspond to configurations of a Turing machine.

Thus Turing arrived at the idea that whatever mental processes are, they can be properly described in terms of Turing machines. Logicians and philosophers have often chosen to see the limitations of computability as an indication that the mind can do something that a machine cannot. Given Turing's original interest in defeating materialism, perhaps it is surprising that he himself made little of his own discovery about this absolute limitation. On the contrary, his interest was more and more on exploring what a machine *could* do, not what it could not. In this direction the 1936 paper held a very important spin-off from his work on Hilbert's problem. The business of following the operation of a Turing machine, of finding out how it will behave at any point, is itself a mechanical process. A machine—a Turing machine—can do it. Thus there exists a type of Turing machine, which Turing called the universal machine, with the property that it can perform any process that could be done by any other

Turing machine; hence, according to Turing's ideas, any mental process. This idea dominated much of his post-war life.

Turing machines become lists of instructions for a single machine, the universal machine, to carry out. As stated in 1936, the universal Turing machine appeared quite unrelated to anything that could be built. But Turing did have a kind of practicality which was quite unlike the spirit of Cambridge pure mathematics. The war gave him his chance. During the Second World War he was Britain's chief cryptanalyst and as such enjoyed great experience with machinery carrying out logical tasks. In particular, the desperate need for faster operations had brought electronics into the picture. In 1944 Turing designed and built his own advanced electronic speech encipherment device. He knew that electronics could make the universal machine into a practical proposition. Of course, now it is easily seen that the practical version of the universal machine is the digital computer. Turing machines become its programmes. By 1945 he wanted to build a first computer—or, as he would say, to build a brain.

Turing was appointed to a position at the National Physical Laboratory with a free hand to design an electronic computer. He proposed a fully worked-out and original hardware design[4]—atoms of logic now becoming practical questions about the components required—but more important, perhaps, was his ability to see in 1945 the potential of programming. The 1936 paper was an important starting-point; it had elements of programming within it. Fundamentally, Turing brought from this logical work the idea that computing involves operations on symbols. These symbols may or may not refer to numerical quantities; in fact, he did not see numerical calculation as at all fundamental. The symbols might as well be instructions as numbers; he saw immediately that the computer could do the work of processing instructions, and thus started on the idea of programming languages.

It is an unfortunate fact that most of his advanced work in this 1945–7 period was lost or wasted; he resigned from the NPL in despair in 1948 when no progress had been made in constructing hardware. His mode of thought and work was quite incompatible with the NPL constraints, and he was unable to manage the situation to the advantage of his project. It is surprising that so little attention has been given to this important topic in post-war British economic history. Later the NPL revived the computer project, and of course other machines at Manchester and Cambridge were also world leaders in their way. But Turing's vision, of advanced programming and hardware developed from the start in harmony, was lost. He never recovered enthusiasm for creating the science of computation, as he certainly could have done if he had so chosen.

However, Turing did not lose interest in the prospect of what he called 'intelligent machinery', or what we would now refer to as artificial intelligence. His ideas were essentially developments of the arguments in the 1936 paper. The 'instruction notes' now become explicit programming, although Turing introduced a new element by attaching much importance to the idea that the computer could modify those instructions according to its experience. But he also wished to apply the 'mental states' idea. To do so, Turing imagined starting with a machine of random structure, and then selecting and reinforcing desired responses to inputs, a process akin to unconscious learning. He saw the development of artificial intelligence as requiring the combination of these ideas.

Turing's work was not full of detailed techniques, or theories of learning; they were manifestos rather than research papers—necessarily so, when the hardware adequate to try out the ideas did not yet exist. But these early papers were very strong on examining underlying concepts. Perhaps the best-known is the 1950 paper[5] which introduces the so-called Turing test. In this, Turing imagines a computer performing so well in response to interrogation, by remote teleprinter, that one cannot tell that it is a computer rather than a person. Then, he argues, one must credit it with thinking.

I feel this thought-experiment is not always properly understood, and Turing should take some of the blame because he introduced the idea in an entertaining but slightly misleading way. He set up the idea of the experiment by first imagining a game where it is a not a machine pretending to be a human being but a man pretending, over the teleprinter, to be a woman. But a moment's thought shows that successful pretence at *this* game would prove nothing. Being or not being a woman is a physical fact irrespective of what anyone says. The point is that, in contrast, Turing held that the successful imitation of intelligence, under the given conditions, *is* intelligence.

The elimination of sight and sound and direct contact from the Turing test conversation is important. Turing's conception of intelligence was that it could be effectively separated from other features and faculties that people have—such as friendliness, charm, or heroism. Reducing contact to teleprinter messages is supposed to perform this separation of intelligence from other qualities. But can these faculties really be separated? Others might give greater weight than

Turing did to the objection that, in any application of general language, words embody concrete connections of the human mind to its environment—social, economic realities—and that these connections are essential to the nature of language.

Turing gave a rather slight reference to this question. But he gave a strong and clear statement of the claim that thinking or 'intelligence' is a process which is properly described within the discrete-state-machine model. It has the great virtue of being a claim that can be pursued experimentally rather than argued about philosophically and of course it has given rise to a large area of research and applications.

Turing's claim also means that it is irrelevant what physical medium is used to embody those states. It is a point to which he constantly referred, although he never looked in detail at the question of relating machine constructions to the quantum nature of matter. At the end of his life, in 1954, he was expressing new interest in the puzzles of quantum mechanics and it is tempting to think that he might have returned to re-examine his early interest in the physical basis of the mind. There is fresh interest now in understanding quantum theory on a deeper level, and in possible connections between the fundamentals of physics and the fundamentals of computation, the field that he opened up. This is uncharted territory. Thus, it is still far too early to know the full significance of Turing's ideas about intelligence.

Notes

1. Turing, A. N. (1937), 'On Computable Numbers, with an Application to the Entscheidungsproblem' *Proc. Lond. Math. Soc.*, 2, **42**, pp. 230–67.
2. Hodges, A. (1983), *Alan Turing: The Enigma*, Hutchinson.
3. For example, Minsky, N. (1967), *Computation: Finite and Infinite*, Prentice-Hall.
4. Turing's computer design, and an important lecture that he gave in February 1947 are reprinted and edited by B. E. Carpenter and R. W. Doran (1986), in Vol. 10 of The Charles Babbage Institute Reprint Series for the History of Computing, MIT Press.
5. Turing, A. N. 'Computing Machinery and Intelligence', *Mind*, October 1950; reprinted in Douglas Hofstadter and Daniel C. Dennett, *The Mind's I*, Brighton: Harvester 1981.

8 The advent of intelligent robots
Michael Brady

Introduction and overview

This chapter is concerned with the subject of intelligent robotics. We shall see that robotics is a broadly based engineering discipline that is advancing rapidly, supported, as it is, by massive funding in the United States, Japan and Europe. By examining the limitations of current industrial robots, I hope to give you some feeling for why robots need to be intelligent.

The systems may surprise you by their engineering sophistication. Note in particular the complexity of the systems integration that is required to achieve complete working robot systems. In passing, I will try to provide a sense of the engineering and scientific underpinnings of robotics. The problems encountered in robotics address fundamental scientific and engineering issues. Currently, however, there is only a glimmer of a Science of Robotics. Evidently, we need to develop one.

I also want to discuss the relationship between robotics and Computing Science because it is precisely the integration of engineering with advanced computing, especially artificial intelligence, that makes intelligent robotics possible.

Toward the end of this chapter, I recount some of my impressions upon returning to the UK after several years' living and working in the United States. Finally, I outline our plans for the development of robotics at Oxford University.

Robots, and why they need to be intelligent

I do not presuppose much background knowledge about robotics from the majority of readers of this article. In fact, I suspect that the average reader's conception of a robot is a mixture of:

- robot 'arms' performing routine industrial tasks such as spray painting, spot welding, forging, and simple assemblies;

*Professor of Information Engineering, University of Oxford.

- automata that never need to rest, never make mistakes, never demand pay rises, and appear to be totally impervious to even the most hostile work environment (not to mention the spectre of unemployment for the work-force who previously performed those tasks); and
- science fiction figures such as HAL in *2001* and R2-D2 and C-3PO in the film *Star Wars*, that are lovable and useful most of the time but have a tendency to turn nasty.

Currently, even the most sophisticated robots in the most advanced research laboratories, are much closer to spot welding and pick-and-place automata than they are to R2-D2. This will certainly continue to be the case for many years to come. Many now in use are, however, probably far more advanced than you might have imagined.

There have been many attempts to define the term 'robot'. By and large, such definitions have been hopeless, since they have simply summarised the state of industrial systems current when the defini-tion was framed. Most notably, consider the widely cited definition proposed by the Robot Association of America: 'A robot is a reprogrammable, multifunctional manipulator designed to move material, parts, tools, or specialized devices, through variable prog-rammed motions for the performance of a variety of tasks.' The definition fails to mention sensing! Robots that cannot sense (more precisely, perceive) their environment inevitably are incapable of modifying their pre-programmed motions to accommodate unex-pected situations, uncertainties such as the varying positions of parts, or non-uniformities in the speed of conveyors. Such robots must be confined to an environment that is perfectly ordered and perfectly modelled. The real world is seldom like that, though the 'perfectly understood world' assumption underlies the application of robots to spot welding, pick-and-place tasks, and spray painting.

A robot that is confined to sensing its environment is seldom of much use. Robots are active devices; they change their environment by performing (hopefully useful) work. The simpler the effectors we equip robots with, the simpler and more circumscribed the actions they can perform. The parallel jaw grippers found on most current industrial robots can pick up conveniently-located, small work-pieces such as computer chips, and they can place them in pre-assigned locations in conveniently-located printed circuit boards. Parallel jaw grippers are not much use if the task is to change a car's distributor, however.

Simple sensors and simple effectors allow a robot to operate successfully in a world that has little uncertainty, and they can work from a simple model of that world. Richer sensors and more dextrous effectors potentially support a wider range of applications and potentially enable a robot to tolerate greater uncertainty. There is a price to be paid for versatility, however, and it is the central theme of this presentation: the robot's model of the world needs to be more complex, and the robot needs to have a greater understanding of it. In short, the robot needs to be more intelligent.

These considerations led me (Brady 1985; Brady and Paul 1984) to coin the following 'definition' of robotics: 'Robotics is the intelligent connection of perception to action'. The definition deliberately avoids mentioning current technologies, such as DC-drives, hydraulic actuators, or silicon computers.

Before we proceed, it is appropriate to issue a note of caution. Since robotics is the field concerned with the intelligent connection of perception to action, artificial intelligence (AI) must have a central role in robotics. Artificial intelligence addresses the following important issues: what knowledge is required in any aspect of thinking; how that knowledge should be represented; and how that knowledge should be used. Robotics challenges AI by forcing it to deal with real objects in the real world. Problem-solving and reasoning techniques and the associated representations developed for purely cognitive problems, often for toy domains, do not necessarily extend to meet the challenge. This theme is elaborated in Brady (1985).

A whirlwind tour of robotics

This section is intended to be a whirlwind tour of the current state of research in robotics throughout the world. Inevitably, much has been omitted. Recent surveys of robotics include (Brady 1985; Brady and Paul 1984; Hanafusa and Inoue 1985; Giralt and Faugeras 1986). The section is organised along the lines of our definition: robotics is the intelligent connection of perception to action. We begin with a section on (visual) perception, follow it with two sections entitled 'From control to thought', and 'reasoning'. We conclude with a section on action.

Perception: robot vision

Purely for reasons of space, we only discuss vision. Other sensory modalities that have been investigated in robotics include touch, sonar, force and proximity (Pugh 1986a; 1986b is a good collection on robot sensors; the other references give sources for the interpretation of sensory data). There are good reasons for concentrating on vision. First, it is by far our most powerful sense, though it is also by far the most complex. Second, vision sensors are the most advanced (though there is considerable room for improvement). Finally, the theory of vision is the most advanced (see Ballard and Brown 1983, Horn 1986; Marr 1984; and Brady 1981).

The first thing to note about computer vision is that it is inherently greedy for computer memory. An image is typically 512 picture elements (pixels) square, and each pixel may represent one of 256 grey levels (that is, each pixel occupies one byte of computer memory). The memory required for one such image is a quarter of a megabyte. Currently popular, multiscale algorithms, for edge detection and stereo, involve as many as eight images, implying two megabytes of computer memory.

Worse, computer vision, especially the early processing stages, is inordinately greedy for processing cycles. Consider, for example, edge detection, which is one of the most important early processing stages and one that has been studied intensively. An advanced edge detector, for example Canny's (1983), may require 10,000 computer operations per pixel, implying 2,500 million operations on a single image! A moderately powerful computer, capable of executing a million operations per second, would take over forty minutes to apply such an edge filter to an image. This hardly constitutes real-time processing! The typical industrial reaction to this observation during the 1970s was to state flatly that vision would never be used in industry. The introduction of simple binary processing around 1978 began to cast doubts upon this opinion. Industrial engineers soon noted the importance of vision and the impotence of binary processing. An alternative reaction to the processing greed of vision was to note that if a separate (relatively simple) processor could be assigned to each pixel, the edge filtering operation referred to above could be performed in a hundredth of a second. Technology approaching this ideal has emerged in the work of Ian Page at Oxford, and of the Thinking Machines Corporation, of Cambridge, Massachusetts.

Although it has been demonstrated to have a key role in shape recognition and three-dimensional vision, edge finding is not much used in current industrial practice. Speed is a major consideration; but it is not the only one. At least as important is the fact that simple edge filters (the ones that are easy to implement efficiently) work unreliably. Edge filters can be designed using modern control and signal processing techniques, and they can be made to run efficiently. Canny's (1983) edge filter is a good example. To design the filter, two measures are defined: first, the signal-to-noise response of the filter, and second, the accuracy to which edges can be localised. These two measures are related by an uncertainty principle. A trade-off between the measures is required. For example, a filter can be developed that optimises their (scale invariant) product. Computer hardware that can compute Canny's edge filter efficiently is under development at Oxford (Page and Brady 1986).

Edge detection is not an end in itself. Its importance is that it makes possible subsequent processing tasks such as shape recognition. It is now possible to recognise (two-dimensional) shapes in cluttered heaps. This is an ability that is beyond current industrial vision and pattern recognition systems that describe objects as collections of global features. Importantly, the systems illustrated in the talk use increasingly complex object models. For example, that developed by Brady and his colleagues is based upon loci of symmetries, and is best expressed using functional analysis and singularity theory.

Notwithstanding these advances in two-dimensional vision, the most important development in computer vision over the past decade has been the demonstration, in research laboratories, of programs capable of three-dimensional vision. Currently, these developments are being transferred into industrial practice. The most powerful of these processes are stereo and motion. The performance of three stereo algorithms are due to: (i) the late David Marr, Tomaso Poggio, and Eric Grimson (MIT); Keith Nishihara (MIT); and Steven Pollard, John Mayhew, and John Frisby (Sheffield) (the algorithm is called PMF). Nishihara has implemented his algorithm in hardware at Schlumberger's Palo Alto Research Center. PMF was developed on an Alvey consortium including GEC. A fourth stereo algorithm, based on an earlier one by Marr and Poggio that was designed as a neural network model, has been implemented on the Connection Machine at Thinking Machines Corporation in Cambridge, Massachusetts. It seems likely that each of the stereo algorithms mentioned here can be executed at 25Hz. Evidently, real-time three-dimensional vision is on the way, both scientifically and technologically.

Turning briefly to motion parallax, an algorithm for determining three-dimensional structure from motion was developed on an Alvey contract at Plessey's Roke Manor Research Centre by Mike Ibison,

Chris Harris, and Len Zapalowski. The algorithm will be combined with Brady's (Brady, *et al.* 1985; Ponce and Brady 1986) work on surface description in another Alvey grant to support path planning and monitoring by a mobile robot.

Industrial three-dimensional vision is currently restricted to the use of a technique known as structured light, which involves triangulation and the active projection of a pattern onto a scene. In fact, the geometry of structured light is precisely that of stereo. The three-dimensional vision processes provide depth at just a few points in an image. Everywhere dense, smooth surfaces are formed by interpolation. Terzopoulos (1985) developed the idea of interpolating such a smooth surface by allowing a thin metal plate to assume its minimal energy configuration after constraining it to pass through the given points. Terzopoulos formulated the problem as a finite element computation, and showed how multiscale algorithms for solving elliptic partial differential equations could be adapted to solve the finite element problem. This suggests parallel execution.

Although considerable progress has been made in understanding stereo, motion, and sonar, no algorithm exists for any of those processes that can generate perfectly accurate depth information in all situations. Perhaps perfect algorithms are practically or scientifically unreachable ideals. The human visual system is notable for its redundancy in that it has over twenty processes for computing three-dimensional structure. Integrating several reasonable processes can potentially perform equivalent to one extraordinarily good process that overcomes the deficiencics of cach.

Three-dimensional objects can now be represented and recognised. We are rapidly reaching the point where the object models used in Computer Aided Design (CAD) can be produced automatically from images. Like CAD models of sculptured surfaces, the representations used in computer vision increasingly rely upon differential geometry and singularity theory. Importantly, differential geometry (in the small) has local support and so curvature tensors can potentially be computed in parallel everywhere on a surface.

From control to thought

There is a continuum of levels of control between the servo-loops that control the individual joints of a robot and systems that plan collision-free paths for a complete articulated robot amongst a sea of obstacles. There is a widespread, though quite mistaken, view that the lower levels of control are quantitative, whereas higher levels are essentially qualitative. In fact, the most advanced path-planning algorithms in existence today work by sliding around on a five-dimensional manifold called configuration space (see Lozano-Perez's papers in Brady *et al*. 1983) to find paths for a single object moving in a sea of static obstacles. The differential topological structures needed to plan paths for multiple moving objects are even more complex.

Just like unsensing robots used for spot welding and intelligent robots, the different levels of control within a single robot are distinguished by the increasing complexity of their models of the world and the increasing complexity of the associated processing. A servo-controller works from a simple representation of the states of its world, and lumps together most of what it does not understand as disturbances. Sometimes, disturbances arise from noise, but often they arise from sources that can potentially be modelled, such as interaction torques.

A trajectory planner may represent the world as a set of positional and force constraints that have to be satisfied. It may represent objects as potential fields where potential is inversely proportional to distance from an obstacle. Trevelyan's sheep-shearing robot (described in Brady and Paul 1984) employs a somewhat more complex environmental model (for the surface of a sheep) consisting of a set of Bernstein–Bezier curves. It uses these curves to plan the motions of its shearing cutter and modifies the planned trajectories on the basis of force and proximity data. In general, the more complex the task to be performed, the more complex must be the system's representation of the world that it inhabits.

The dynamic equations of a six-degrees-of-freedom, open kinematic chain (the conventional robot arm) consist of six second-order differential equations. Throughout the 1970s it was assumed that solving them in full was computationally intractable. Robot servo-control was based on simplifying the equation of motion, typically by dropping several of the terms. Usually, the velocity-dependent (Coriolis, centripetal, and gyroscopic) terms are dropped (which is why industrial robots are driven at much slower speeds than they are mechanically capable of). In 1981, it was shown that the dynamic equations could be formulated in a way that exhibited a natural recurrence structure. This has enabled the full kinematics and inverse dynamics for an n-degree-of freedom arm to be computed in $O(n)$ steps. On a conventional microprocessor, this enables the full kinematics and dynamics to be computed in about one millisecond.

The simultaneous control of force and position is poorly understood. Recently, it has become clear that much is to be gained by applying non-linear, self-tuning control to the multivariable systems that consist of consecutive parallel joints of industrial robot arms. We plan to investigate these issues, as well as the control of flexible arms, at Oxford.

Reasoning

The highest levels of robot control involve complex geometric models. Often, reasoning is called geometric reasoning to emphasise the point. The use of complex, articulated geometric (CAD) models of objects distinguishes path planning from more abstract artificial intelligence planning systems. Path planning is a reasoning problem that is generic in the sense that many other problems can be shown to be equivalent to instances of it. Examples include: packing silicon devices onto a chip; laying out furniture in a room; and realising task-level robot programming.

Other examples of geometric reasoning use the methods of Collins and Wu to maintain dependency networks between assumptions and conclusions. For example, suppose we assume that an image has been formed using orthographic (parallel) projection. When are the de-projections of lines that are parallel in the image also parallel in space? A program developed by Joe Mundy at GEC's Corporate Research and Development Center in Schenectady, NY, can figure this out. Suppose we later confess that the projection was in fact perspective. Mundy's program can elaborate its reasoning to find the extra cases (none of which are thought of by vision programmers and all of which cause programs to crash). The Alvey project entitled 'Design to Product' studies similar issues.

Action

Remarkably few kinematic structures have been explored in robotics. One novel design is embodied in the GADFLY robot developed by John Streeter and his colleagues at the Marconi Great Baddow Research Centre. The parallel kinematic structure of the GADFLY, which closely resembles a flight simulator, makes the GADFLY remarkably stiff, which in turn makes it ideal for certain kinds of assembly.

Indeed, every industrial robot arm to date has been designed to be stiff (though the results in many cases leave much to be desired).

Often, however, flexible arms would have massive advantages. They tend to be light, to have much greater power-to-weight ratios than their inflexible counterparts, and the passive compliance inherent to their structure makes them more suited to assembly. The problem is that they are difficult to control. The snake-like robot constructed by Bob Cannon at Stanford illustrates the complexity involved in controlling a flexible robot. A number of flexible arms are under construction in the Robotics Group of the Department of Engineering Science of Oxford University. In particular, a two-link robot, developed by Ron Daniel and his colleagues, is controlled by communicating servo-systems, one controlling position, the other controlling force.

We turn now from arms to hands. The arguments in favour of dextrous hands are summarised in Brady (1985). Several multi-fingered hands have been developed over the past three years. Peter Taylor of GEC's Great Baddow Marconi Research Centre has constructed a four-fingered hand whose associated stiffness tensor can be altered to control grasp. A three-fingered robot hand and associated control system has been developed by Ken Salisbury, first at Stanford University's Artificial Intelligence Laboratory (in association with JPL) and subsequently at the MIT Artificial Intelligence Laboratory. The emphasis of Salisbury's project is on hierarchical, general stiffness control of grasping. A four-fingered hand has been developed by Steve Jacobsen, John Woods, and their colleagues at the Biomedical Center of the University of Utah, in collaboration with the MIT Artificial Intelligence Laboratory. The thrust of the MIT-Utah system is on kinematic design and actuation. A multi-processor control system is under development at MIT.

Developments have also been made with walking machines. An example of this is a biped walking machine developed by Hirofumi Miura (1984) and his associates at the University of Tokyo. This was the first statically unstable, dynamically stable biped walking machine to be developed.

A series of running machines also have been built by Marc Raibert (1986) at the Robotics Institute of Carnegie-Mellon University. Raibert's work emphasises balance rather than gait as the fundamental component of walking and running. An important side-effect of Raibert's work has been to show how complex control systems can be built up from smaller ones by exploiting principles of symmetry. Perhaps we will never see running machines in our factories. I would not be surprised, however, if the control system architecture invented by Raibert, and the crucial role played by symmetry, did not illustrate important general principles. Surely, this is the essence of Engineering Science.

Finally, we turn from legged to wheeled machines. First the HILARE mobile robot system developed by Georges Giralt, Raja Chatila, and their colleagues at the CNRS Laboratoire d'Automatique et d'Analyse des Systemes in Toulouse. Recently, an autonomous land vehicle has been developed by Martin-Marietta in Colorado as part of DARPA's Strategic Computing Programme. MELDOG, built by Tachi at MITI's Mechanical Engineering Laboratory (MEL) in Tsukuba City, Japan, shows that the science and technology of mobile robots can be applied to the problem of making robot guide dogs for the partially sighted.

Postscript: intelligent robots and animate intelligence

Robotics is deeply linked to the study of human perception, cognition, and motor control. To be sure, it is not necessary to solve problems the way that humans do, and efficiency will always dictate novel, special-purpose designs. It is doubtful that calculators use the same algorithms for arithmetic that humans do, that airplanes use the same technique to fly as birds, or that horses need roads. Nevertheless, in many cases, the underlying problem to be solved is the same, irrespective of whether it is to be solved by man or machine.

For example, how do we develop a theory of grasping and stability of grasp? An important step is to build dextrous hands; but how? One idea is to model the human system. The MIT–Utah hand does precisely this. It is the nimblest hand built to date. Assuming that it is decided to build a hand consisting of two fingers opposing a thumb, what is the optimal angle between the thumb and the fingers? Salisbury and Craig formulated this problem using the variational calculus and found that the answer was almost exactly the same as that adopted by humans. Evidently, evolution is good at mathematics.

As a second example, how do we see depth using stereo? Area correlation, the technique developed by applications engineers, works poorly when there is little texture but strong edges. Currently, the best stereo algorithms were inspired by known facts concerning human stereovision. The PMF algorithm, for example, exploits the notion of disparity gradient, shown by Julesz and Burt to apply to human stereo. The disparity gradient limit employed in Pollard's implementation is based on that estimated for human vision.

How do people execute straight-line reaching motions? Hollerbach has shown that a model developed for robot trajectory planning provides a remarkably close fit to data obtained from human motions. How do people compute intensity changes in images? Parker and Hawken have shown that a slight variation on the difference-of-Gaussians model pioneered in speech research, and subsequently championed in vision by Wilson, provides a close fit to measurements from cells in human visual cortex.

Robotics research and human perception and motor control stand to gain much from each other. At Oxford, there is a close community involving the Departments of Engineering Science, Psychology, Physiology, and the Program Research Group that shares seminars and has authored joint research proposals.

Plans at Oxford

Initially, our research will be concentrated in four areas: image processing and understanding; the development of an autonomous guided vehicle; manipulator design and control; and sensor design.

Research in image understanding will focus on theories of two- and three-dimensional shape to enable robots to recognise objects and to navigate among a sea of obstacles. We shall build upon our previous work on smoothed local symmetries and intrinsic surface patch representations. A project, funded by the Alvey Directorate, involves collaborative research with the Plessey Roke Manor research centre and is intended to monitor path execution for a robot moving through the environment modelled as a collection of surfaces. Image-processing research involves the development of two parallel processors; one a refinement of Ian Page's rasterop processor, the other a pipelined convolver supported by IBM.

The autonomous guided vehicle (AGV) project builds on the vision work, but involves several other components: sensor integration; hierarchical, multivariable, sensor-based control; geometric reasoning; and systems integration. The AGV project will be carried out jointly with the Rutherford-Appleton Laboratories. Industrial sponsors include BP, GEC, RAL, Thorn-EMI, and RSRE.

Research in manipulation and control is currently focused on the development of flexible, lightweight arms. These pose formidable control problems. Dr Ron Daniel and his colleagues are studying two complementary issues: compliance and speed. The work is supported by CEGB and SERC.

Work on sensing includes a range sensor invented by Jim Allan, a GEC Research Fellow, that is based on laser interferometry. The work is funded in part by the National Engineering Laboratory. In other work, a structured light sensor to be attached to a robot wrist is under construction.

Robotics and computer science

Intelligent robotics is not possible without Computing Science. Conversely, robotics poses a difficult, and potentially important, challenge to the development of Computing Science, in that first it necessitates complex interactions between computers and the real world; second, it requires computer systems that can reason about physical objects and physical processes; and third, it demands parallel computation for the practical implementation of its science.

Interacting with the real world

Over its first thirty or so years, Computing Science has (naturally) been mostly concerned with internal problems such as the development of programming languages and operating systems and the technology of their implementation. Similarly, the theory of computation has been concerned with internal problems, such as sharpening the definition of computability, the semantics of computing constructs, and the complexity of algorithms for data-processing operations such as sorting and mathematical operations such as multiplication and matrix inversion. Robotics offers an opportunity to Computing Science to turn outward to the physical world of real objects and processes.

Against this background of solipsism, it is no surprise that input and output have often been regarded as an unwelcome though necessary evil in Computing Science. For example, they were largely ignored in the original definition of Algol 60; a pattern that has been repeated in programming-language design many times since. The previously second-class status of input and output was raised to first class by Hoare (1978). He showed that certain communications primitives formed an elegant, yet powerful, basis for programming complex non-deterministic systems as groups of communicating sequential systems. Similarly, input and output, in the form of perception and action, are two of the three critical components of robotics. Robotics is a natural application in which to develop models of programming such as Hoare's, for its inherent concern with physical processes promises a severe test of computational realisations of the idea of process.

The languages that are used to program robots have not been affected much by advances in Computing Science. Language design for robotics is far from trivial, however. The difficulties that have to be overcome include: scheduling interactions with sensors; guaranteeing real-time execution of commands by a servo system; supporting multiple representations of rotations and positions; representing sensory data; and resolving positional and force constraints on robot trajectories.

Reasoning about physical objects and processes

The behaviour of physical processes can be modelled in many different ways, not all of them mathematical. Injection moulding of plastic or the operation of a cylinder in an internal combustion engine is usually modelled by partial differential equations, which are solved numerically using finite element techniques. Finite element methods are still poorly understood, especially when the mesh has to be updated automatically to reflect changing shape with time.

Much simpler models suffice for many assembly operations, which can be idealised as point contacts and analysed using classical mechanics. Friction complicates the story since it renders mechanics non-deterministic. Nevertheless, we can often predict fairly well how a flat object lying on a rough table will move if it is poked by a finger, though the problem was ignored by nineteenth-century applied mathematicians. Along these lines, Mason has shown how simple models of friction can be exploited in assembly and in fixing the position and orientation of moving objects.

Sometimes mathematical modelling is not appropriate. A seven-year-old child has no difficulty using a rusty screwdriver to unfasten a worn screw, though the mathematics required to model the situation are extremely complex and his knowledge of classical mechanics and the finite element method is often slight. Evidently, the seven-year-old represents the physics of the situation naively. An important concern of artificial intelligence is to understand such naive models and the reasoning they support.

To reason about physical objects and processes requires representations. Hopcroft and Krafft (1985) have summarised the challenges: general representational models must be

- abstract enough so as not to require computationally infeasible deduction;
- formal, so that reasoning about objects is possible;
- structured, so that complex physical objects and processes can be understandably represented; and
- complete, or at least strong enough that an interesting set of objects and tasks can be modelled.

They survey approaches to geometric modelling, showing how none are wholly satisfactory. For example, the bicubic patches that are often used to render surfaces in Computer-Aided Design (CAD) systems are degree 18 surfaces, which appears to preclude the use of algebraic methods for reasoning about bicubic splines.

Current CAD models are of limited usefulness for robot reasoning. Imagine trying to determine whether a polyhedral model of a screw fits a similar model of a nut, given that the numbers of faces involved in each model are numbered in the thousands, and that the planar facets are densest and the fit most poorly conditioned at the more highly curved portions such as the threads. More abstract representations of objects, developed in artificial intelligence, are needed to support such reasoning. The Alvey Design-to-Product project, conceived by Popplestone, addresses some of these important problems.

Computer graphics, vision, robot navigation, CAD, and reasoning about physical objects and processes are deeply related through computational geometry. For example, in his recently completed thesis at Essex University, Meng Er has shown that a (dual-space) representation that enables mechanical drawings to be interpreted also provides the basis for a fast hidden line graphics algorithm. Models and machining are inevitably inaccurate and positions gleaned from sensors are uncertain. This complicates the task of reasoning systems.

A workshop that brings together researchers in robotics, vision, CAD, reasoning, and specifications to explore these issues was held at Keble College, Oxford, in July 1986. It was financially supported by the SERC ACME Directorate and by the US National Science Foundation. The proceedings will be published as a book to draw attention to the issues and to encourage research in the area.

The challenge of parallelism

Intelligent robots are positive gluttons for processing cycles. As we pointed out earlier, low-level vision algorithms take far too much time on a conventional microprocessor. The light at the end of the tunnel is parallelism. During the 1970s, the cost of hardware made computer vision infeasible. Now, science is lagging behind technology, for while VLSI (Very Large Scale Integration) has made massive parallelism feasible at reasonable cost, few novel parallel architectures have been proposed, and, more significantly, there is little in the way of a theory of parallel computation.

We noted earlier that parallelism is crucial if advanced computer vision algorithms are to be a part of industrial practice. Vision is a natural application for parallelism because many computations have local support. This is obviously true of convolution and thresholding. What is less obviously true, but true nevertheless, is that a global state can often be computed through local interactions executed in parallel. This can be applied, for example, to compute shape from shading, shape from contour, structure from motion, and to interpolate dense surface maps from sparse data. These problems are discussed in Horn (1986); and Ballard and Brown (1983).

There are fledgling theories of parallel computation in vision. Poggio has noted that many vision algorithms are mathematically ill-posed and require additional smoothness assumptions if they are to be solved. Regularisation theory, originally developed for optimal control, generalises least-squares techniques to variational problems, which provides a valuable mathematical underpinning for many vision problems. Regularised computations are straightforwardly implemented on parallel, neural networks, such as Boltzmann machines, that avoid some of the difficulties associated with linear classifiers. It should be pointed out, though, that the apparently exponential convergence rates of Boltzmann machines, and the apparent lack of concern for convergence in studies of 'connectionism', point to inadequacies of current theories.

Turning from perception to action, we noted earlier that the kinematics and dynamics of a robot arm can be formulated 'recursively'. This suggests pipeline architectures that can compute the full dynamics of a six-degrees-of-freedom arm in under a millisecond. Orin (in Brady and Paul 1984) has designed a VLSI circuit that serves as a robot joint processor in such a pipeline architecture.

Finally, several research efforts are underway aimed at designing parallel computers to support reasoning. Examples include the Alvey Alice project, the parallel Prolog machine at ICOT, and the connection machines under development in the USA.

Nurturing robotics science

Following the more technical discussions of the previous sections, we now turn to more philosophical issues. In this section we note some of the institutional implications of the inter-disciplinary nature of robotics and say why stop-go funding cycles must be avoided. We conclude with some reflections on research collaborations between universities and industry.

Robotics is inter-disciplinary

It is evident from the above discussions that robotics draws upon many disciplines. Robots are articulated electromechanical devices whose complex dynamics and changing inertias make them difficult to control. Robots bristle with devices that sense force, proximity, position, and range. Computing Science is fundamental to robotics, especially artificial intelligence. Finally, we have much to learn from human perception and motor control. By any measure, robotics is an inter-disciplinary subject. Because of this, robotics research is normally a team enterprise, where the team members have specialist skills in particular areas complemented by sufficient breadth to work together effectively.

Unfortunately, effective collaboration across departmental boundaries is often made difficult by rules, regulations, and prejudices. Departmental leaders need to be aware of this if robotics research is to be encouraged. At major universities in the United States, interdisciplinary interaction is facilitated by a distinction that is made between departments, which organise teaching, and laboratories, which organise research. The members of a laboratory are often drawn from several departments and housed together. Day-to-day contact between members of a research team encourages the establishment of a corporate indentity, builds *esprit de corps*, and improves research productivity. We recognise and practise this within a department; the arguments are equally compelling, but the administrative problems more challenging, for research efforts that cross departmental boundaries.

Stop-go funding cycles must be avoided

Research funding for artificial intelligence was hard to come by in the 1970s. The situation was most bleak around 1978, when I, and several of my colleagues, emigrated to the United States 'for good'. Ironically, we left just a couple of years before the tide began to turn. The Alvey Report, and its subsequent implementation, has wrought remarkable changes.

An unfortunate legacy of the 1970s drought, one that was noted in The Alvey Report, was the lack of a sufficient number of talented young researchers towards whom the step increase in funding could be directed. The worst effect of the 1970s drought was not the emigration of established researchers *per se*; but the consequent 'missing generation' of PhD graduates.

Funding droughts are not restricted to the UK. In the late 1970s, 'robotics' was a term that could not be mentioned in research proposals to the Department of Defense, even in the proposals of leading groups such as the MIT Artificial Intelligence Laboratory. Some robotics research was supported, but only by subterfuge, and only with the connivance of far-sighted funding agents in DARPA and ONR. When MIT greatly expanded its effort in 1982, it faced the same problem as the UK in artificial intelligence: a lack of graduates and a lack of graduate applications.

As a result of the Alvey initiative, graduates in information technology are now being produced in increasing numbers, and several highly productive research groups have been established with reasonable equipment and good relationships with industry. It is to be hoped that we have learned that people are the scarcest resource in information technology. Surely we have also learned that it was the lack of critical mass research groups that most distinguished British (and European) research in IT from that in the USA.

Another 'stop' cycle of funding will quickly undo what has been achieved, and will destroy the delicate growth of IT in the UK. Young plants can benefit from pruning; but pruning has to be done carefully if a seedling is to survive. The plans for Alvey II recognise this, and it is hoped that they will receive effective support from all parties.

Not all of the signs are reassuring. The overall volume of the information technology industry world-wide was estimated to be $500 billion in 1984, of which the UK share was about $4 billion. Unfortunately, the UK industry operates at a deficit of about $1 billion. Moreover, whereas the IT industry world-wide is growing at about 25 per cent per annum, the number of jobs in the UK is falling. The number of electronics graduates in the UK has fallen from 2,700 in 1984 to about 2,300 this year, and the trend is downwards, as indeed it is in most sectors of higher education. Japan has twice as big a population as the UK, and the US population is four times the UK's; yet total spending on R&D during 1982–3 in Japan and USA was almost three times and seven times that of the UK respectively. Whereas national expenditure on R&D grew by about 7 per cent in Japan, and 4.6 per cent in the USA, it fell by 0.9 per cent in the UK.

Relationships between industry and the universities

Since my return to the UK I have visited over two dozen British companies, and about ten universities. Relations between industry and the universities have changed markedly in the past five years, to the benefit of both parties. The Alvey initiative has been most successful in encouraging this new climate of research collaboration. Long way may it continue and flourish!

On my travels, I encountered some groups that stressed the short-term nature of their work, and emphasised the importance of dealing with the nitty-gritty of practical shop floor problems. This was to be expected, especially from industrial applications engineers. What was not to be expected was that some of these groups were in universities. Equally unexpectedly, but to my delight, several companies disapproved of 'shop-floor realism' and lectured me on the need for universities to concentrate on basic research to be exploited five to ten years out.

There is, naturally, a need for balance and a need for work across the entire spectrum that stretches from extreme short-term problems to long-term basic research. We must, however, support basic research, if only for simple practical reasons. If robotics research had accepted the decree that 'vision is useless' during the 1970s, there would be no industrial vision now. There is, in fact, very little in the UK. If robotics research were now to accept the judgement that three-dimensional vision modules such as stereo and motion are inherently too expensive, so that research on them has no practical basis, there will be no industrial three-dimensional vision in the UK five to ten years from now either. Similarly, without support for basic research, there will be no systems that perform geometric reasoning, process planning, and there will be no dextrous hands and flexible arms. There *will* be in Japan, the USA, and continental Europe.

Currently, world-class basic research is being carried out in the UK, especially in vision, control, and geometric reasoning. We perform much worse than the USA, Japan, and certain European countries in technology transfer. Universities have an important role to play in technology transfer, not least by training staff on industrial secondment. American and Japanese companies give sabbatical leave to employees that are marked for rapid promotion. Every middle-level manager of every Japanese company I know has spent at least one year in an overseas research laboratory. A year's worth of research plus a generous 'bench fee' to the host institution is a small price to pay for learning the ways of working and thinking of a world-class laboratory.

Robotics and society

The status of engineers

Consider Table 8.1, supplied to me by John Taylor, Director of Hewlett Packard Bristol Research Centre. Note that the USA and Japan each produce about seven times as many engineers as the UK. With a population twice that of the UK, Japan has eight times as many undergraduates as the UK.

We need to improve the number of high-quality engineers in our society. How can we attract the finest brains into engineering, especially information engineering? There are two aspects to this. First, we must increase the number of students following technical courses in our schools, and we must improve the quality of that education. Any decline in the interest and quality of preparation of science

Table 8.1. Engineering Graduates World-wide

	Japan	USA	UK
Grad. Engineers per year (thousands)	75	70	10
Grad. Engineers per thousand pop.	0.64	0.30	0.18
Grad. EE per year (thousands)	19	16	2.5
Grad. EE per thousand pop.	0.16	0.068	0.04

students at school must presage a similar decline in higher education and industry.

Second, we need to raise the status of engineers in our society. The fundamental problems of robotics discussed in this chapter are as deep and challenging as those of mathematics and physics. Indeed, their solutions depend, for the most part, upon an understanding of the appropriate mathematics and physics. Nevertheless, mathematics and physics have considerably greater status than engineering in the UK. Proportionately, the UK produces about six times as many scientists per engineer as Japan.

Unemployment and the static society

Robotics is associated in many peoples' minds with unemployment. Unemployment is already wastefully high in the UK. Surely, we should reduce funding levels for robotics, to avoid exacerbating the tragedy of unemployment?

No purpose is served by pretending that some job categories will not disappear because of robots, in the sense that the work will be turned over to robots. Analogously, the development of automobiles reduced the need for industries that supported horse transportation. Between the third quarter of the nineteenth and the second quarter of the twentieth centuries, there was a sharp reduction in the number of people earning their living as stable lads, ostlers, and blacksmiths. Meanwhile, vastly more car workers, road workers, mechanics, and garage attendants were employed in the entirely new job categories associated with the new technology.

The same applies to the development of computers. Forecasters in the early 1950s predicted vast unemployment in banking, accountancy, and clerical work. Quite the opposite has taken place. Computing employs tens of thousands of people in entirely new job categories, many more than were displaced. Whole job categories disappeared, to be replaced by entirely new ones in an expanding economy. Computing and automobiles are now the mainstays of the American economy.

There is no evidence to suggest that the same will not be equally true of robotics and automated manufacture. People needed to be retrained to work on cars and computers. Similarly, we need to retrain people to work with robots and in automated manufacture. Manufacturing processes are changing rapidly. Decreasing numbers of workers in manufacturing will stay with the same job throughout their working lives. The age of the gold watch after a lifetime of service is rapidly passing. With luck, work, and good management, robotics and automated manufacture could be the basis for substantial growth in our economy and society.

Acknowledgements

This article has been improved by the comments of my colleagues at Oxford: Ron Daniel, Mike Irving, Kevin Warwick, Ian Page, Jim Allan, Dave Clark, Tony Hoare, Dave Foster, Dave Forsyth, Tony Fraser, Vaughan Michell, Greg Provan, and Ron Cagenello. Naomi Brady provided the 'intelligent layperson' perspective on the paper.

References

Ballard, D. H., and Brown, C. M. (1983), *Computer Vision*, Englewood Cliffs, NJ: Prentice-Hall.

Brady, Michael, ed. (1981), *Computer Vision*, Amsterdam: North-Holland.

Brady, Michael, (1985), 'Artificial Intelligence and Robotics', *Artificial Intelligence*.

Brady, Michael, Asada, Haruo, Ponce, Jean and Yuille, Alan (1985), 'Describing surfaces', *Computer Vision, Graphics, and Image Processing*.

Brady, Michael, and Paul, Richard, eds (1984), *Robotics Research*, (Proceedings of the First International Symposium, Bretton Woods, NH), Cambridge MA: MIT Press.

Canny, J. F. (1983), 'Finding edges and lines in images', MSc thesis, MIT Artificial Intelligence Laboratory.

Giralt, Georges and Faugeras, Olivier (1986), *Robotics Research* (Proceedings of the Third International Symposium, Gouvieux, France), Cambridge, MA: MIT Press.

Hanafusa, Hideo, and Inoue, Hirochka (1985), *Robotics Research* (Proceedings of the Second International Symposium), Kyoto, Cambridge, MA: MIT Press.

Hoare, C. A. R. (1978), 'Communicating sequential processes', *Comm. Assoc. for Comput. Mach*.

Hocroft, John E. and Krafft, Dean B. (1985), 'The challenge of robotics for computer science', Cornell University memo.

Hillis, W. Daniel (1985), *The Connection Machine*, Cambridge, MA: MIT Press.

Horn, B. K. P., *Robot Vision*, Cambridge, MA: MIT Press.

Marr, D. (1983). *Vision*, Freeman.

Miura, Hirofuma (1984), 'Dynamical walk of biped locomotion', *International Journal of Robotics Research*, 3(3).

Page, Ian, and Brady, Michael (1986), 'The Arrow Processor', Oxford University, March.

Ponce, Jean and Brady, Michael (1986), 'Towards a surface primal sketch', in Takeo Kanade (ed.), *Three-Dimensional Vision*, Academic Press.

Pugh, Alan, ed. (1986a), *Robot Sensors: Vision*, Vol. 1, IFS.
Pugh, Alan, ed. (1986b), *Robot Sensors: Tactile and Non-vision*, Vol. 2, IFS.
Raibert, Marc (1986), *Machines That Run*, Cambridge, MA: MIT Press.
Terzopoulos, Demetri (1985), 'Computing visible surface representations',
    PhD thesis, MIT Artificial Intelligence Laboratory.

9 'This is a very unpredictable machine': on computers and human cognition

Janni Nielsen

The general picture which emerges from much research dealing with children and computers is that children are motivated and do not encounter severe problems when learning programming (Papert *et al*. 1979; Papert 1980; 1981; 1984, Noss 1983a; 1983b; 1985; Watt, nd.). The impression is that programming challenges higher mental functions, and the children acquire the ability for systematic structuring and develop procedural thinking. The implication is that their learning process is osmotic, that is they learn mathematics and programming without knowing that they learn 'like learning French by living in France . . . without being taught' (Papert 1980, p. 4). It is argued (Larsen, 1984) that the systematic procedure and the necessity of dealing with the rigour and formalism which are essential in programming should enhance procedural thinking. Thus Papert (1980) suggests getting children to do 'the turtle', for example walk a circle when they have problems in programming a circle; or to write a program which will simulate juggling with balls before actually attempting to juggle. By acquiring the ability to break down reality to the simplest possible elements and organise the elements in a sequential and temporal process, children may develop higher cognitive skills, and acquire procedural thinking.

Not only programming, but also word-processing systems may further this cognitive development. By separating structure from content, Lawler (1980; 1985) introduced a simple word-processing system to his daughter. The structure—or the systematic temporal procedure built into the system—functioned as a pre-programmed composition for writing stories. Lawler suggests that by working within this systematic procedure, the structure was gradually acquired

*Psychologist, the Royal Danish School of Educational Studies, Copenhagen, Denmark.

by the child, and became the structure within the frames of which she, several years later, generated her writing. Thus it seems that the systematic procedure for organising knowledge—or the procedural thinking as the frame for cognitive development—was acquired by the girl.

Noss's (1983a; 1983b; 1985) point of departure is different. According to Noss, children already structure their knowledge and their thinking is logical. It is the same logical processes that working with mathematics demands, he says. But as mathematics is abstract and decontextualised, this has hitherto been difficult for children. With the computer and LOGO, however, it has become possible to present the formalisation of mathematical thinking in a concretised way. This is the advantage of the computer, and children simply have to apply the same structure and logic they have developed in every-day life to computers and mathematics.

Thus learning to program and work with computers seems to mean learning to deal with rigour and formalism, with reality reduced to its simplest possible elements, structure separated from and independent of specific content, and decontextualised symbols. Writing programs becomes a sequential process by applying a temporal structure, and through this developing higher cognitive skills, thus acquiring procedural thinking.

Children and computers

The research is very promising, yet in my research many of the teenagers[1] did not get very far during the one year[2] I followed them, despite the fact that they are much older than many of the children in the research mentioned, and presumably have reached a higher level in cognitive development (Piagetian).

For a start, many of the pupils were not very enthusiastic about working with the computer. One pupil expressed his views quite clearly: 'I think if somebody *really* wants to do it, they should be allowed to. I don't, it doesn't interest me.' Several concurred with his view. Others would simply sneak away from the classroom during the sessions, or pretend to be very occupied with pencil and paper, making sure this pretence would last for the whole computer session. Still others would flatly refuse to work with 'these ridiculous machines'. The pupils found it tiresome to work with the computer, because it was extremely time-consuming. One of them said working with the computer was 'terribly boring; quite honestly I could do it more quickly with pencil and paper', and staring at the screen made one 'heavy in the head'. The work tended to become tedious because it seemed meaningless: 'What is it for . . . I don't understand anything'; and thus it was found 'too difficult'. Even the few pupils who were capable of writing programs which would execute fairly complicated patterns, found it tedious 'because it is all the same'.

However, at times their attention would be held by the patterns which emerged on the screen. They were fascinated by the movements. When this happened, they would improvise, build on associations and create beautiful patterns: 'If we draw a line there, it can be used to . . . I will write my name inside and put it on my door . . .'. They clearly let themselves be inspired by the graphics, and a beautiful drawing became important. One may speak of creative production, which demands a specific qualification: the ability to let oneself be seduced by the object and its uniqueness. That is, not to impose structure or methods from above, but let oneself be open to the material one is working with, producing by means of feelings and perceptions, but of course within the limits posed by the technique (Nielsen and Roepstorff 1985). And they would try to get some meaning out of what they were doing, by making it a product which could be used for something, or simply by suggesting that it looked like something else. When this happened they found working with the computer exciting. But often, their creativity was curtailed by problems with the programming, and motivation tended to disappear. 'Lets not bother' suggested Jane. Susan was willing to go along, but then she remembered the teachers and continued, 'because if they ask to see it (the product) it is going to be a bit difficult' (Nielsen 1986). One did not work so much in order to gain knowledge, but more in order to meet the requirements of the school.

Many of the pupils had problems with reducing reality to the simplest possible elements. A good example was when they had to break down the movement of actually walking a circle. Despite the help of the teacher, many pupils did not voice it as a process of step, turn a little, step, turn a little, and so on. Moreover, once this was explicitly verbalised (in most cases by the teacher) the pupils still had difficulties in organising these components into a sequential process and writing a program in accordance with the temporal logic. The pupils did not naturally walk a circle like a turtle. On the contrary, the process of walking a circle was perceived and executed as an organic whole. They may, of course, come to learn to reduce reality to fragments, but to the pupils it was a very specialised approach, or method, which did not come naturally.

To Susan and Jane, working with decontextualised symbols did not come easily. Many—but not all[3]—did not seem to carry any meaning. The functions the orders caused were abstract and took place out of sight, and could not be seen, felt or executed by the girls. As words carried no meaning, the girls also had problems in systematising the programming orders in accordance with the a priori defined temporal structure. But the girls had heard something about 'being systematic' and 'structure'. So, to be on the safe side, they automatically and very systematically typed the following sequence: CATALOGUE, FORGET, END, GRAPHIC, CLEAR, REMEMBER—whenever they left a program or a drawing. And they were not the only ones to use this systematic procedure, though the sequence of the orders could vary.

The pupils also found the necessary temporal organisation difficult. Structuring information, or structuring thoughts into a priori defined patterns did not come easily. When the computer failed at the eleventh attempt to produce a triangle on the basis of a program where REPEAT had to be used, Michael concluded: 'This is a very unpredictable machine'. Michael and John had five REPEAT in their program. The road to knowledge was not organised in accordance with procedural logic: 'Lets see . . . make it big . . . type . . . mm . . . FORWARD (30) . . . yes and then we have to . . . mm . . . mm . . . turn? . . . Yes turn . . . try, . . . type 120 and then we want it to . . . It is not big enough, we should have made it bigger . . . it has to go down (30) and then . . . Hey we have to use this REPEAT . . . O.K. REPEAT(6) . . . that's it'. When the program did not work the boys started correcting it by adding more REPEAT, then removing order lines—at one point, and after many attempts, John suggested that they remove the name of the program—and finally they ended up with 5 REPEAT. Their thoughts clearly moved along other tracks, they could not restrict them to the formalism and rigour essential in programming.

Not only the sequence of and the relation between the orders, the temporal logic, was found difficult. Many of the pupils also experienced difficulties with the relationship between the program and the graphics. They did not seem to have mental images of what a written program would execute: 'Did we make that?' asked Susan, astonished. 'Apparently . . . we ordered it to do it' answered Jane with surprise in her voice. 'Finally we succeeded', stated Susan, and the girls laughed happily. They had produced the drawing shown in Figure 9.1, but the instruction was: Use your program TURN (Figure 9.2) and change the right order turn of the triangle, so the six

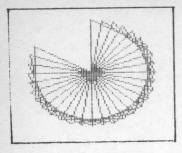

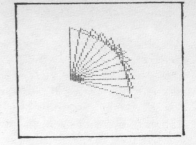

Figure 9.1   **Figure 9.2**

triangles will form a secant (Nielsen, 1986). However, something was drawn on the screen, there was a visible product. Thus the girls, as many of the other pupils, concluded that the problem was solved.

Learning programming and mathematics did not come about as a 'fingertip effect' (Perkins 1985). The pupils in my research had problems in learning to reduce reality to simple components, to acquire the structure, the temporal logic, and organise the content within this framework. They had problems working with decon-textualised symbols, and development of higher cognitive skills in terms of procedural thinking did not seem to occur, though there did not seem to be anything wrong with their logic. The logic Susan expresses when she continues with the problem-solving is very real, and may be termed real logic, derived from everyday life, from laying hands on reality.

Thus the children in my research did not fit the general picture. A picture, though it also deals with children's programming problems and may be very much alive and expressive in its concrete examples, nevertheless leaves one with the impression that children—fairly easily—develop higher cognitive skills. In the results which are put forward there seems to be an implicit assumption of the road to knowledge, to cognitive development, as an organised, structured, logical and rational approach. Moving within the frames of the research cited would almost unavoidably lead to the conclusion that the children in my research were very unfortunate. But there were so many of them, and it became obvious that the model of human cognition had to be questioned if these pupils were to be understood. A point of departure for this is the knowledge ideal, the question of the road to knowledge.

Changes in the knowledge ideal

Procedural thinking as the framework for cognitive development emerges, more or less explicitly, as the ideal—an ideal which is not new and which may be approached in a very illustrative way by setting it in a historical perspective. The questions of how and what one may know something about may be viewed fruitfully within the frames of the changes in the knowledge ideal in science.

Obviously, the knowledge ideal in education is not the same as the scientific ideal. However, the ideal in education, that is, what knowledge, hence which qualifications, it is considered essential for children to acquire and how this cognitive development may be ensured, must be understood not only as a result of actual societal conditions (the computer as an example) but also as a product of historically developed knowledge traditions. As a general frame for the knowledge ideal in society, and thus also for education, stands the historically produced scientific ideal.[4] which indicates the road by which knowledge may be obtained. A sketch of this may serve as a frame for our understanding.

Plato formulated an idealistic philosophy in which the real world was the world of ideas. Knowledge, or cognition, about the world could mainly be acquired through the liberation of the thought from the body, and the road to knowledge went through the renunciation of sensuous lust.[5]

Aristotle, the founder of logic, considered philosophy the ultimate form of the human mind. The world of concepts grew out of the perceived reality, that is, concepts were founded in matter, and made up logical classes. The road to knowledge went through the active reason which was characterised, not by being liberated from the body, but by exercising control and curbing the forces of the sensuous body.

But it is not until the seventeenth-century scientific revolution that the philosophical or scientific ideals are radically reinforced. With Bacons's inductive method the scientific ideal became experimental[6] rather than theoretical, and its goal was control of and mastery over nature. With Descartes' soul/body division, expressed in his famous credo, *Cogito, ergo sum*, the scientific researcher as an objective cognisant being was 'created', and man's separateness from the knowable established. These scientific ideals were gradually founded in the societal universe of interpretations, and became the frames within which the relation between human and world was interpreted.[7]

The scientific ideal which emerged must also be understood in relation to societal changes, just as the essential role of political and economical forces in the development of science must be taken into consideration (Kuhn 1973). But for now, my interest is the concepts through which the world was grasped and the road to knowledge perceived.

The new scientific ideal was established on the basis of, and at the same time conditioned a change from a holistic organic world-view, to a reduced mechanical inorganic world-view. Originally, nature was perceived as feminine, as a nourishing giving mother in a coherent universe characterised by equilibrium, and to meddle with nature would bring about disturbances in the existing balance of the cosmos. With modern science, however, Mother Earth was neutralised and conceptualised as an object, a mechanical object which could be made the subject of interventions.

The transformation from an organic world-view to an inorganic, mechanical one was not without its detractors. The debate on the growth of mining activities may serve as an illustration of this. The opponents of mining stressed that 'The Earth does not conceal and remove from our eyes those things which are useful and necessary . . . SHE brings into the light of day the herbs, vegetables, fruits . . . The minerals on the other hand SHE buries far beneath in the depth of the ground, therefore they should not be sought' (Merchant 1983). The defenders of mining argued that 'Nature has given the Earth to man that HE might cultivate IT, and draw out of IT's caverns metals' (ibid.). With modern science nature became something which man could subdue to his will: 'I am come in very truth, leading to you Nature with all her children, to bind her to your service and make her your slave' (Bacon, in Keller 1985).

The aim of the new science was man's mastery of nature, and according to Henry Oldenburg, Secretary of the Royal Society, this could only take place by creating 'a Masculine Philosophy whereby the Mind of Man may be ennobled with the knowledge of the solid Truth' (Keller 1985).

The essential characteristics of science became reductionism, objectivity and logical rationality, expressed in the methodical approach; 'rational, experimental inquiry, unhindered by prejudice, wild speculations and emotional outbursts, was considered the only path to success' (Easlea 1981).

The pure reason

As a parallel to the development of the mechanistic world-view, a gradual change in the view of human beings also took place and eventually came to rest in the scientific knowledge ideal. With the objective, rational, reductionistic and logical science in the 'royal' seat, the road to knowledge could not be reached through the subjective, the emotional and the sensuous dimensions in the human being. Rational thought—the pure reason—took over. The ideal human became a reason-driven, logical and objective cognisant being. Repression of the more spontaneous emotional, sensuous and subjective human qualifications was felt to be desirable. As mentioned earlier, this ideal does not belong solely to the seventeenth-century scientific revolution, but runs like a red thread throughout history. But it is with the scientific revolution that the notion of pure reason as the driving force in the development of knowledge becomes the ideal.

Of course, the subjective, emotional and sensuous dimensions could not be repressed fully in man. Yet we find that the change led to a gender polarisation in the human ideal. To be logical, rational and driven by pure reason was made the masculine ideal, and ascribed to the man; while the subjective, emotional and sensuous dimensions came to make up the picture of the feminine ideal, and were ascribed to the woman—though not as qualifications: on the contrary, to possess these dimensions was considered dequalifying. Women were viewed as intellectually inferior to men because, 'women's brains were less powerful than men's ... women were considered to be less rational than men, more emotional than men, more subject to passion' (Easlea 1981). The masculine ideal, hence the qualifications deemed essential in the pursuit of knowledge and science, were ascribed only to men. But the feminine dimensions were considered embodied in both man and woman. For woman this was her destiny, and it was used to legitimise the restriction of her room for development, of her practical activities to husband, children and home, and to legitimise her exclusion from 'higher' knowledge in schools and institutions of learning such as universities. 'The females, through the cold and moist of their sex, cannot be endowed with so profound a judgement [as men]: we find indeed that they take with appearance of knowledge in sleight and easy matters, but seldom reach any farther than to a sleight superficial SMATTERING in any deep science' (ibid). Man, however, could and should liberate himself from these destructive forces. 'The Woman in us still prosecutes a deceit, like that begun in the Garden. And our Understandings are wedded to an Eve, as fatal as the Mother of our miseries' (Joseph Glanwill, in Easlea 1981). Man would be far from the 'Tree of Knowledge', unless all feminine characteristics were excluded from the true philosophy.

Thus, in the naming of the world, in the construction and understanding of reality and in the construction and understanding of the human being as intelligent, a development has taken place which may be characterised by a growing polarisation of the objective and the subjective, which also shows itself as a polarisation of the masculine and the feminine. In the dimensions ascribed to the feminine ideal, negative connotations are embedded, the ideal becomes devalued, and to a growing degree repressed. Whereas the dimensions ascribed to the masculine ideal become ennobled as the ideal. With the scientific revolution, the relation between man and nature may be characterised by a radical division between the knower and the knowable. The way to knowledge becomes masculine, only to be obtained by man, an autonomous, rational logical cognisant being, disconnected from nature. This is also true of nature, the sensuous emotional forces in man himself which must be subdued—thus man's connectedness with his self disappears.

A consequence of this development has been not only an exclusion of women from science, but also—as a tendency—an exclusion of the feminine universe of interpretation as an essential tool for describing, interpreting and conceptualising the world. But more than that, it has meant repression of the emotional and sensuous qualifications. They are considered irrelevant for the development of science, and for the road to knowledge, the consequence of this being that subjectivity has been denied and repressed too. It is objectivity which is produced.

Of course, subjectivity can never be fully repressed, though the neutralisation in the naming of the world may lead one to believe so. Form and content in much scientific production is decisive. Research design, methods and results are presented within the frames of a formalised structure, in a complex self-referring language and in symbols (graphs and statistics, for example) in which it becomes difficult to find the picture behind the picture of reality which is being represented. Not to mention reality itself. The subject, the researcher himself has almost disappeared. Subjectivity, like Mother Nature, has become invisible; they no longer appear in the naming.

Man-made technology

The computer is both the connecting link and the offshoot, or rather the result of the merging of technology and science. In a sense, the computer is a child of mathematics. Constructed on the basis of mathematical logic, pure logic, it can only process information within these frameworks. Information which is to be stored and processed in a computer must be systematised and structured according to the rules and principles of formal logic. There can be no ambiguity if the computer is to function; the concepts must not be diffuse, as they cannot be made the object of interpretation. Thus information must be reduced to data. This reduction also holds true for the language which is used. No matter how much it is attempted to make programming language natural, it is still an artificial language. It may be characterised as unambiguous, static and independent of context, whereas natural language is characterised by its ambiguity, its relation to the concrete world, and its dependence on context, thus being dynamic (Nielsen and Roepstorff 1985).

Of course, in principle, all information may be stored in a computer. But not all information can be processed, at least not immediately. A picture can be transmitted, that is copied. The same applies to symbols—letters, words, etc. But none of them can be processed unless they are allotted a meaning. The computer can only process that which may be represented unambiguously, in a digitalised form. Obviously, not much in the world or in nature is unambiguous or digital, but one may reduce reality. Once reality has been reduced, processing in a computer can only take place according to the rules and principles of the data logic.

Reality, that of which we may know something, has been reduced to data. And the road to knowledge and cognition has to pass through the computer, the wedge between the world and the human. The computer becomes the means through which knowledge of reality may be acquired, thus the knowable and the knower subject and object, have become radically separated.

The computer acts as a mediator and interpreter between the human and the field of knowledge. It is, at the same time, a technology which ignores the specific content domain and demands that the knowledge field be reduced to its simplest possible elements, in accordance with the principles of data processing, and organised in an a priori defined sequential procedure, thus a technology that structures and defines matter, that of which we may know something. It is also a technology which comes to play an essential role in how knowledge may be acquired, because programming can only take place within the rules and principles for data processing. A procedural process demanding that the human being organise and structure her/his thinking in accordance with this.

The computer, one may say, is a mechanical 'being' which logically, rationally and objectively deals with a reduced reality. The computer is considered by some people intelligence itself. Though an artificial intelligence, it is, and this is important, liberated from the muddle of emotions, senses and subjectivity. With this 'cognitive' computer, then, the masculine ideal has been reached.

We know more than we can say

Working from the model of procedural thinking, or the masculine ideal, as the road to knowledge, one is left with a limited picture of children's work with computers. The model does not make it possible to grasp the qualifications, and the creativity which comes into play when the pupils move beyond the limits imposed by the computer. When learning programming, children do not sit in front of the computer as if they were small learning machines. On the contrary, they do many other things, which all together play an important role in the learning situation.

But the model also has to be further extended if the manifold qualifications the pupils apply when working with the computer are to be understood. Human beings are, in their pursuit of knowledge,

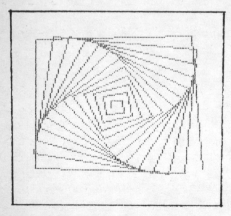

```
SPIRAL(A)
FORWARD(A)
RIGHT TURN(88)
SPIRAL(A + 1)
END
```

Figure 9.3

much more manifold and creative than the 'cognitive' computer. Cecily and Tanya had just copied from the exercise sheet, and seen executed a program which drew a spiral, at the same time making it bigger (Figure 9.3). The girls did not fully understand how the program worked, but they were very excited by the figure it drew, and had it printed out. They then had to write a program which would turn a triangle around, at the same time making it bigger and bigger. At first, the girls looked completely lost—they did not know where to begin. Finally Cecily started to dictate very hesitantly, and Tanya went along with the typing, noting that they were guessing. What Cecily did was to copy the spiral program, changing only the name of the program to TT(A) and the right turn order to 120. The first attempt looked like this:

```
TT(A)
FORWARD(A)
RIGHT TURN(120)
SPIRAL(A + 1)
END
```

Obviously, the program did not produce the planned figure. However, seeing the program executed, paying close attention to the movements on the screen, the girls gradually came to realise that a program for the triangle had to be written first. Although the girls did not reason directly that the triangle is a closed figure, whereas the spiral is open, so that a new program for the triangle had to be written, they seemed to have perceived something along these lines, by looking closely at the screen. In the next attempt, when they used the REPEAT procedure, they had some problems with the angles and the number of REPEATs, but eventually got around to the right solution. Still the planned figure was not executed: 'It keeps drawing Squares, why does it do that?' asked Cecily with pain in her voice, rubbing her hands over her face. Realising that they could not solve this problem, the girls asked for help, and the teacher explained that the TT(A) program had to call itself, not the spiral. But Cecily and Tanya did not understand, to them SPIRAL(A+1) meant 'turn and get bigger'. Thus they had not understood the specific structure, nor the relation between the orders in the program. Yet it was this program that they hesitantly, but intuitively, had taken as point of departure. The girls almost succeeded, but they could not verbalise what they did , nor explain why. It became clear that it was not the program, but their image of it, that they seemed to build on. By drawing on their visual impression of the movements, they seemed to have perceived an undetermined relationship between the SPIRAL program and the turning triangle, and they were capable, in the process of writing and correcting the TT(A) program, of piecing together the elements. Step by step, and on the basis of the visual knowledge hitherto acquired, they almost managed to write a correct program.

But how could this happen? The program was not written on the basis of a clear conceptualisation of the programming orders, the relation between these and the functions they caused, and the logic the girls applied cannot be termed procedural—or formal. It seems more appropriate to speak of a logic of associations, many of which could not be verbalised. This is because not all knowledge may be explicitly verbalised, or, to put it another way: we know much more than we can say, and in our attempts to acquire knowledge, we move along many roads.

Human cognition

Thus, in order to understand Cecily and Tanya, it is necessary to extend the model of how knowledge is acquired, because human cognition embodies much more than symbols (language) and formal logic. Or rather, human beings draw on both the qualities which historically have come to be named masculine and feminine respectively, that is the senso-motor and the emotive and symbolic cognitive ways. Only in theory can these be separated; in practice they are integrated, and the basis for cognition, for a person's comprehension of a coherent world, throughout life.[8]

The senso-motor way of cognition is based in body and senses. It is qualified through the individual's practical activities, that is, by laying hands on reality. The emotive cognitive way grows out of and is qualified through the necessary emotional relations formed with other humans. Emotions function as an orientating means for a person's way of relating to the world, and by qualifying this cognitive way, the possibility for dissolution of borders between self and other—for caring identification—is created. Neither of these two cognitive ways enjoys a high status in our culture. To a large extent they are—as pointed out—demarcated as essential means for cognitive development. However, they cannot be suppressed entirely, and continuously rear their heads, their strength being that they may demolish borders and be point of departure for transgressing activities.

The symbolic cognitive way may be understood as the ability to let the world be represented by words (it could of course be colours, music, etc.), to allot a meaning to the symbols. Language, if founded in human relations, and in the mother–child interaction (the ideal model), moves from being merely sounds to the child, to become the naming of the interaction. Through the use of language in many different situations, the sounds become differentiated, they are allotted a meaning and gradually become concepts. But not uniquely defined concepts, because there are no sharp borders in everyday life, but blurred, deriving their meaning from the context in which the emotive and senso-motor dimensions are embedded.

The process of concept formation may be illustrated thus:

$$\text{process of concept formation} \begin{cases} \text{tacit} \\ \text{symbolic} \end{cases}$$

The tacit dimensions, or tacit knowledge (Polanyi 1976), are understood as the senso-motor and emotive cognitive ways. Obviously, part of this knowledge may become verbalised, but it is essential that we keep in mind that we know much more than we can say. In our cognition of reality, we draw on tacit knowledge, part of which is indeterminable.

The symbolic, which is seen here as language, serves two functions. It is a means of communication, but it may also become detached from human interaction. Through language one may transgress the immediate, voice past and future, create theoretical constructions, and so on. As such, language becomes an essential—but not the only—tool for the intellect. But in order for our mental speculations not to become merely figments of the brain, they must have reality as point of departure, and they must, in turn, be confronted with reality, with context.

Yet language may become detached from context to the extent that it becomes a pure abstraction. When nothing embodies language, when no senses nor human relations hold it, it becomes without reference, and it must be defined, and rules and principles for its use must be made. It becomes signs, like mathematics and computer language. This does not imply that these signs cannot be used as tools, but they must be applied in a qualitative way.

To return briefly to Cecily and Tanya, it is tacit knowledge which the girls mainly drew on when constructing the program. They had perceived an indeterminable relationship between the Spiral program and the Triangle program. By relying heavily on visualisation, when

constructing the TT(A) program, moving forwards and backwards
between graphics and text, perceiving an indeterminable relationship
in the information they came across, they almost succeeded. The
visualisation, or rather the senso-motor cognitive way, was the important—but not the only—factor in the process. Thus the program
could not written without the teacher's help, the emotive cognitive
way based on human interaction. Emotions also extended to the
problem the girls were working with, in the sense that without a
positive orientation towards the problem, the motivation would have
disappeared. But also the symbolic cognitive way played a role:
without some understanding of the concepts used, motivation would
have suffered. When concepts appear meaningless there is nothing to
hold on to, the purpose of the activity is lost, and it becomes difficult
to maintain an engagement. Maybe motivation did tend to disappear,
because the girls were not enthusiastic about the work, and only went
to the computer reluctantly. As Tanya said, 'If somebody really wants
to do it they should be allowed to. I don't'. But the girls were very
disciplined, they worked, like Jane and Susan, mainly to meet the
teacher's requirements. And one may speak of an instrumental
approach, or instrumental motivation.

Other roads to knowledge

But other pupils did not. As mentioned earlier, some would simply
sneak away from the sessions. Others stayed, but did not work with
the computer. Tom and Louis took their point of departure in the
technology which was present. The pupils were videotaped during
their work with the computers, and the boys used this technology to
transform the classroom into a radio station, and by doing this they
drew their subjective experiences, their everyday life, into the learning situation. Also here one may speak of associative thinking, where
the here-and-now situation (the technology and the classroom) was
linked with the life outside. I would suggest that we may speak of a
creative approach where feelings and perceptions were a point of
departure for the production. The radio station was made by hanging
the earphones of Tom's personal stereo on the video microphone.
Tom would announce rock music with a very suggestive speaker
voice, and then turn up the sound. Louis acted as cameraman, making
sure of shooting Tom in the centre of the picture. Synthesised music,
drums and weeping guitars, music speaking with and to the body and

the emotions exploded on the videotapes. Of course this is also what it is all about for these teenagers with so many changes taking place in their bodies, with the emotional confusion of being neither child nor adult. But the creativity of the boys may be perceived as more than that. They speak with and to the opposite of that which is on the agenda. Thus their reaction may also be perceived as a protest against the meaningless, against this suppression of the subjective emotions that they experience. But more than that, by referring to feelings and senses they point to something essential—that these are other ways of acquiring knowledge which should not be overlooked.

It is the same creativity—though applied within the framework of the technology—which the girls use, when they name the programs after their boyfriends. They try to maintain something meaningful by letting the concept, the program name, refer to a specific context—a love affair. By applying the names they also maintain these other cognitive ways, because it is body, senses and emotions—caring for the other—that love is all about. These qualifications—which children posess in abundance—should not be suppressed and restricted to love for another human being. Barbara McClintock, a 1983 Nobel prize winner, has very clearly demonstrated how these other roads to knowledge may further scientific discovery. For her, it was essential to 'hear what the material has to say to you . . . the openness to let it come to you', but more than anything it was fundamental to have 'a feeling for the organism' (Keller 1983). There are many roads to knowledge, and by using different ones,—by complementary approaches (Bohr 1957)[9] one may come to know.

But the argument for the other cognitive ways may be carried even further. Whether or not children come to master programming, the message conveyed to them in today's education is clear: the method for treating information, reducing the world to elements and organising according to formal logic, is the goal. Thus procedural thinking is *the* approach in order to acquire knowledge, and children learn that the emotional, sensuous and subjective approaches to the world are of little value.

Yet, in the future, it is the children and the qualifications they so richly possess that we shall be in need of. Not experts, who, through a process of calculation, mechanically produce scientific results. Unless these other approaches to knowledge of the world are qualified, we may come no further than the man of Cheng who measured his foot, put the measurements away and then went to the market in order to buy himself a pair of shoes. When he found the shoes he wanted, he realised that he had left the measurements behind. He never got his shoes, because he 'trusted the measurements more than my own foot' (Roberts 1979).

The ideal embedded in science and technology—two forces upon which a continually more controlling role has been conferred—carried within it, along with its undeniable success also the means of destruction. It has brought about the continuing production of nuclear weapons in a constant arms race (though we already have enough to destroy the world several times over), pollution of sea and lakes, acid rain killing forests, smog, and so on (Capra 1981). It has also served as the foundation for the development of an industry and work processes in which the sensuous, emotional and living human being is reduced to a mechanical object.[10] Meanwhile millions of people—most of them children—die of hunger every year, hundreds of millions are undernourished, and almost two-fifths of the world's population do not have access to the most basic of medical care (Capra 1981). This destructive development, which may be counteracted by experts and scientists, must also be counteracted by other human beings. The point of departure for knowledge and ways of dealing with reality are not necessarily adequate because it is founded in a specific scientific approach; it may be equally adequate if founded in emotive and senso-motor cognitive ways—though these also need to be further qualified.

Notes

1. 44 pupils, 14–15 years of age, working with a Danish variation of LOGO in mathematical education, in a state school in suburban Copenhagen.
2. Approximately 44 hours of programming.
3. When working on the graphics some of the orders, or rather the function of the orders was immediately visible, and working with these did not seem to create problems.
4. Historically science and technology are two forces in society upon which a continually more controlling role has been conferred.
5. That is: man's (*erastes*) road to knowledge—not woman's—went through the renunciation of the lust—for another man (*eromenos*).
6. This experimental approach in science is characterised by limiting the field under investigation to the smallest unit possible, and keeping the chosen variables under strict control. By changing the influence of variables one may acquire knowledge of the specific field and make predictions.
7. In borderlines, for example in art or narrative literature, the opposite poles existed, but not as deciding forces in society.

8. For a detailed presentation and discussion of this cognitive model, see Nielsen and Roepstorff (1985).
9. Bohr stated this in relation to an epistemological problem in quantum physics. Though other knowledge domains differ from quantum mechanics, complementary approaches are also necessary in these areas.
10. The taylorisation of the work process.

References

Bohr, Niels (1957), *Atomteori og menneskelig erkendelse*, Copenhagen.

Capra, Fritjof (1982), *The Turning Point*, London: Fontana.

Easlea, Brian (1981), *Science and Sexual Oppression*, London: Weidenfeld and Nicholson.

Keller, Evelyn Fox (1983), *A Feeling for the Organism—the Life and Work of Barbara McClintock*, San Francisco.

Keller, Evelyn Fox (1985), *Reflections on Gender and Science*, New Haven, CT: Yale University Press.

Kuhn, Thomas (1973), *Videnskabens Revolutioner*. Fremad.

Larsen, Steen Folke (1984), 'Kognitionens logikker' *Psyke & Logos*, 2, pp. 221–243.

Lawler, Robert (1980), 'One Child's Learning: Introducing Writing with a Computer, LOGO Memo no. 55', Massachusetts Institute of Technology.

Lawler, Robert (1985), *Computer Experience and Cognitive Development, A Child's Learning in a Computer Culture*, Ellis Horwood, NY.

Merchant, Carolyn (1983), *The Death of Nature—Women, Ecology and the Scientific Revolution,* Harper & Row.

Nielsen, Janni (1986a), 'Not the Computer but Human Interaction—is the basis for cognitive development and education', *Education and Computing*, Special issue.

Nielsen, Janni (1986b), ' "I trusted the measurements more than my foot", said the man', Paper presented at Information Technology and Education, Plovdiv, Bulgaria, 9–12 October.

Nielsen, Janni and Lisbet Roepstorff (1985), 'Girls and Computers—a World of Difference?' Contribution to the Third GASAT Conference, Kingston, England, pp. 64–80.

Noss, Richard (1983a), 'Beginning LOGO in the Primary School: Exploring with a Floor Turtle', AUCBE paper no. 1, Chiltern Project (England).

Noss, Richard (1983b), 'Learning with LOGO—Is the Teacher Necessary?', AUCBE paper no 2, Chiltern Project (England).

Noss, Richard (1985), 'Creating a Mathematical Environment through Programming: A Study of Young Children Learning LOGO', PhD thesis University of London, Institute of Education.

Papert, Seymour, Watt Daniel, diSessa, Andrea and Weir, Sylvia (1979), 'Final Report of The Brookline Logo Project', LOGO Memo no. 53, Massachusetts Institute of Technology.

Papert, Seymour (1980), *Mindstorms. Children, Computers and Powerful Ideas* New York: Basic Books

Papert, Seymour (1981), 'Computers and Computer Cultures', *Creative Computing*, 7, 2, pp. 82–8.

Papert, Seymour (1984), 'Computer as Mudpie', *Classroom Computer Learning*, **4**, 6, pp. 37–40.

Perkins, D. N. (1985), 'The Fingertip Effect: How Information-Processing Technology shapes Thinking', *Educational Reseacher*, **14**, 7, pp. 11–17.

Polanyi, Michael (1968), 'Logic and Psychology', *American Psychologist*, **23**, pp. 27–43.

Roberts, Moss (1979), *Chinese Fairy Tales and Fantasies*, New York: Pantheon Books.

Watt, Daniel (n.d.), 'A Comparison of the Problem Solving Styles of Two Students Learning LOGO: a Computer Language for Children' LOGO group, Massachusetts Institute of Technology.

10 Creativity, intelligence and evolution

Euan Macphail

Creativity in animals?

Although my main academic interest centres on the very general question of how intelligence has evolved, I was inspired by Richard Gregory's title for the theme of this book, 'Creative Intelligences' to reflect on the narrower question of how creativity evolved. Somewhat to my surprise, those reflections have led me to conclude that creativity did not evolve; that animals—by which I mean non-human animals—are not creative, and that creativity emerged fairly abruptly with the arrival of *Homo sapiens* in the world.

Animals do, of course, create many things which human beings find beautiful, and it might seem that we must inevitably conclude that those products reflect the creativity of their makers. Let me take some examples involving birds, as I shall concentrate on avian work when I go on to discuss intelligence in general.

Male bower-birds build a variety of large and structurally complex bowers with which they hope to attract female bower-birds. To make the bowers more attractive, they decorate them with coloured objects such as fruit, berries and flowers. The structures they create are attractive not only to female birds, but to humans also. Does the activity of the male bower-bird differ in any important way from that of a human involved in, say, painting a picture? If the human is creative, is not the bower-bird also?

In an attempt to tackle such questions, consider now the tail of a peacock. That, too, is a complex, beautiful structure whose function is to attract females. But do we suppose that the peacock is being creative when forming its tail? Surely not, any more than we suppose that a rosebush is when producing its flowers. The question now becomes, does the bower-bird's making of its bower differ from the peacock's growth of its tail in a way which would allow us to suppose creativity in the bower-bird?

*Senior Lecturer in Psychology, University of York

One important difference might seem to be that there are more differences between the bowers made by individuals of a given species than there are between the tails of peacocks of the same species. The trouble with accepting these differences as examples of individual creativity is that it is perfectly reasonable to assume that the variation amongst bowers reflects such uninteresting facts as differences in the local availability of materials. There is no reason to suppose that any individual bower-bird would consistently make more beautiful bowers, given comparable materials and site, than any other bird of the same species, and so, no reason to suppose that differences between bowers reflect differences in talent or taste between individual birds.

Although different individuals create different bowers, the birds of a given species of bower-bird (and there are eighteen species of bower-bird, of which twelve actually build bowers) all make similar bowers in the sense that they are all distinguishable from the types of bower made by other species. The general design of a bower is, then, species-specific. What is more, the more elaborate the bower of a given species, the less elaborate is the (male) plumage of that species. In other words, plumage and bowers are in a sense behaviourally exchangeable. And this leads me to the conclusion that in building bowers, bower-birds are unfolding behavioural patterns encoded in the genes of their species, just as peacocks unfold a genetically-coded morphological pattern in forming their tails.

Similar arguments apply, I believe, to essentially all the species-specific products, whether behavioural or morphological, of animals. The argument hinges on the claim that animals are not original in those creations, however beautiful we may find them. There are individual differences, but no reason to suppose that they arise from the exercise of any creative capacity. But, of course, to conclude that animals' 'spontaneous' behaviour is not creative is not the same as to conclude that animals are not creative. If we cannot find evidence of creativity in their natural environment, perhaps we should look instead at their responses to novel behavioural demands, to see whether we might find signs of creativity in 'unnatural' situations.

Evolution of intelligence

Just as the species-specific behavioural attributes of animals enable them to adapt to those features of the environment that are relatively constant from one generation to the next, the learning capacities of animals allow them to adapt to changes in the environment which occur unpredictably and over a much smaller time-scale. So that when we ask about the capacity of animals to adapt to novel 'unnatural' environmental demands, we are asking about their ability to learn, to solve problems—in other words, about their general intelligence. Do animals, then, differ in their learning abilities, and how did our human intelligence evolve?

My answer to those questions is one which, perhaps, does not accord with suppositions which are fairly widespread. I began by surveying the available experimental literature on learning and problem-solving in non-human vertebrates (and here I narrow the definition of animals still further, to exclude the invertebrates which form in fact the overwhelming majority of animal species). Contrary to my expectations, I was unable to find any convincing evidence of superiority in problem-solving in any one group over any other. There were, of course, many tasks which one group could solve and another could not, but, equally, no reason to suppose that a group which could not perform a given task failed because of a deficit in intellect rather than because of a difference in some other factor affecting performance such as perception, motor skill or motivation. In the absence of evidence to the contrary, it has been my argument that we should conclude that all non-human vertebrates possess the same intellectual capacity: in other words, that there is no gradual ascent in intellect from fishes through amphibians and reptiles to mammals, from non-primates to primates, and finally to man. A goldfish is as intelligent as a chimpanzee, and a pigeon as bright as a dolphin.

This is not the place in which to go through my case in detail, since that would require discussion of a wide range of experiments using many different species. I can, however, illustrate the argument by describing experiments which bear on two corollaries of the 'null hypothesis'. The first is, that some supposedly 'lower' species may be more intelligent then we might anticipate; the second is that the achievements of some supposedly 'higher' species may not in fact be the intellectual feats that they appear to be on the surface. In each case, the experiment of primary interest involves pigeons, and the focus on pigeons is particularly appropriate in this context: the pigeon intellect is not unusually highly regarded, and pigeons do not belong the 'highest' order of birds, the passerines (to which the crow family—widely believed to contain the most intelligent birds—belongs).

Insight in pigeons?

Wolfgang Koehler carried out a number of experiments using a colony of chimpanzees on the island of Tenerife, on which he was virtually imprisoned during the First World War. In one of the best-known of these experiments, a banana was suspended from the roof of a room in which the chimpanzees were contained, out of reach of the animals. In another part of the room was a wooden box. All the six chimpanzees in the room began by leaping up at the fruit in vain attempts to reach it. One of them—Sultan—abandoned those efforts, paced restlessly up and down, and then abruptly went over to the box, moved it to within reach of the banana, climbed onto the box, and seized the banana. The suddenness of the solution and its consequent smooth performance convinced Koehler that it was an example of 'insightful' problem-solving. We are not concerned here with the question of the occurrence or otherwise of 'insight' but with the question whether some supposedly less intelligent species—the pigeon—might not also solve the problem.

It is clear that pigeons could not solve the problem precisely as set for chimpanzees, and equally clear that the reasons for that have nothing to do with the pigeon's intellect. Pigeons do not eat bananas, would not be strong enough to move the box, and can in any case fly. So what we need to know is whether a pigeon could solve some analogous problem which posed the same intellectual demands but which did not make impossible demands of the pigeon's motivational and muscular systems. Recently Robert Epstein of Harvard University described just such an analogue (see Epstein *et al*, 1984).

In Epstein's experiment, pigeons were intially taught two habits. In some sessions, pigeons were rewarded with food for pushing (with their beaks) a small cardboard box towards a green spot on the wall of their experimental cage. The spot was at different points in different sessions, and the pigeons therefore learned what might be called 'directional pushing'. In other sessions, the box was fixed in position in the same cage, directly below a small plastic banana suspended from the roof of the cage. The bird was trained to peck the banana for food reward while standing on the box; if the pigeon jumped or flew at the banana, it was not rewarded. The pigeon therefore learned in these sessions to climb onto the box to peck the banana, and not to attempt to fly at it.

In the test stage of Epstein's experiment, the box was placed in the cage at some distance from the banana, and there was no spot on the wall of the cage. The performance of the pigeons was remarkably similar to Sultan's—they began by making vain efforts to stretch up to peck the banana, indulged in restless pacing to and fro, and finally, according to Epstein: 'each subject began rather suddenly to push the box in what was clearly the direction of the banana. . . . Each subject stopped pushing in the appropriate place, climbed, and pecked the banana (Epstein *et al.*, 1984).

There are, of course, many differences between the Epstein and the Koehler experiments. One particularly striking difference should, perhaps, be discussed here, and that is, that the pigeons, unlike the chimpanzees, were specifically trained to move the box directionally. But other workers have shown that chimpanzees do not solve problems involving the manipulation of objects unless the animals have had extensive previous experience with the objects, so that this difference does not seem of significance to the intellectual demands made by the problem on the two species. The behavioural repertoire available to the pigeons and to the chimpanzees was comparable, and the mode of solution achieved in each case was similar. However we may suppose that the chimpanzees (or, to be precise, Sultan, the one chimpanzee that *did* solve the problem) proceeded in the solution, it seems plausible to suppose that the pigeons' intellectual processes followed the same course. So that, if this task demonstrates insightful problem-solving then pigeons, like chimpanzees, are capable of insight.

Spontaneous communication between pigeons?

The principal point of my second example is to show that superficially complex performance may sometimes emerge from basically rather simple intellectual mechanisms.

In 1972 a BBC *Horizon* programme showed a film which demonstrated 'spontaneous communication' between two dolphins. The dolphins were placed in tanks alongside each other, and were prevented from seeing each other by an opaque barrier between them. One dolphin could see a panel which was from time to time lit with one of two visual stimuli, which we can call S_1 and S_2. The other dolphin found two paddles at the end of its tank. The experimenter introduced the simple rule that if the first ('sender') dolphin saw S_1, then a push on the left-hand paddle by the other ('receiver') dolphin obtained food reward for both dolphins and pushes on the right-hand paddle had no effect; and if the sender saw S_2, a response by the receiver on the right-hand paddle would obtain rewards, and responses on the left paddle had no effect. Without any further explicit training, the dolphins succeeded in obtaining reward on virtually all presentations of S_1 and S_2: in other words, the sender dolphin was communicating with the receiver dolphin in such a way as to enable the receiver dolphin to choose correctly.

Robert Boakes of the University of Sussex was intrigued by this demonstration and eventually succeeded in providing an analysis of the communication involved, an analysis supported by an analogous experiments conducted, using pigeons, with his colleague Ilse Gaertner (see Boakes and Gaertner 1977). In their experiment, Boakes and Gaertner placed two pigeons in adjoining cages, and separated them with a transparent screen—the pigeons could, then, unlike the dolphins, both see and hear each other. The sender pigeon saw a small circular panel on which either red or green light occasionally appeared. Although the receiver pigeon could see the sender, it could not see the coloured stimuli, since there was an opaque screen which obscured the panel from the receiver (but not from the sender). The receiver pigeon saw two response keys which were lit with white light six seconds after the sender's panel had been illuminated at the start of each trial. The rule was that if the sender saw a red light, then the receiver should peck the left key to obtain food reward for both birds, or the right if he saw the green light. As the experimenters had anticipated, the pigeons, like the dolphins, mastered the problem, and performed consistently at levels well above chance: the pigeons, that is, communicated. But how is their performance best character-ised? Dr Boakes's analysis indicates that the communication involved is of a distinctly restricted and impoverished nature.

First, consider the receiver. This animal begins by obtaining a series of rewards and non-rewards seemingly unrelated to which of the two possible responses it chooses to emit. Numerous experimen-ters have found that many species—both avian and mam-malian—tend in such circumstances to adopt a 'position habit': that is, they simply select the same side for response (for some individuals the left, for others, the right) on all trials. This is, of course, a perfectly rational strategy in response to what appears to be an insoluble problem.

Now suppose that the receiver has adopted a position habit and consider the sender's position. Because of the rules of the game, the sender will now find that reward consistently follows presentations of one colour, and non-reward, presentation of the other colour. Previous work has shown that pigeons will approach (and peck) a signal for food reward, and withdraw from one signalling no food. Back now to the receiver, who will now see the sender approaching the key on some trials, and withdrawing on others; and it will soon learn that the trials on which the sender withdraws are those on which its response is not followed by reward. Thus the receiver will tend to withhold pecks from the key on its preferred side when it sees the sender withdraw; this in turn provides the necessary condition for responding to the other, non-preferred key, which is in fact the correct key on the trials on which the sender withdraws. The problem is solved.

We can now reflect on the interaction between the two birds. The sender pigeon is reacting differentially to the two colours, which is all the information that the receiver needs: but the sender is not communicating in any intentional sense, it does not 'know' that it is communicating—its differential responding is a direct consequence of the adoption by the receiver of a position habit. Boakes and Gaertner (1977) were able to analyse the behaviour of different pairs of pigeons in detail, and to show that this analysis did in fact apply, and that the degree and stability of the solutions achieved were explicable in terms of their analysis. No such empirical analysis of the dolphins' performance is available, but it seems, to say the least, likely that their solution was achieved in a similar way: by the receiver adopting a position habit, and by the sender consequentially emitting different sounds on seeing each of the stimuli—perhaps something akin to a squeal of delight when seeing the stimulus followed by reward, and a groan when seeing the other stimulus?

Association formation and causality

The two examples that I have discussed in some detail above will, I hope, have given a flavour of the type of experiment carried out by comparative psychologists, and may also have helped show why I remain unconvinced of the intellectual superiority of some species over others.

The general conclusion that all non-human vertebrates possess the same intellectual capacity suggests that the mechanisms of learning in vertebrates may be relatively simple. A brief digression here may help to show that simple mechanisms might nevertheless prove extremely powerful in enabling anaimals to adapt to novel stimulus conditions. One capacity which all vertebrates clearly possess is that of forming associations. Now although we tend to think of association formation in a context of arbitrary pairings of such unnatural stimuli as bells and food pellets, in the real world regular pairings of two events normally reflect the existence of a causal link between the events. So that an animal which possessed a device for detecting regular pairings of events—an association-formation device—would in fact detect causal links. If we see association formation as a process which unravels the causal networks within an animals's environment, we can see that such a process, although in a sense simple, could indeed be extremely efficient in predicting future events. I am not arguing that association formation is the only learning process available to animals, but I would argue that association formation, along with some few other similarly 'simple' processes, might indeed be sufficient to explain all non-human intellectual activity.

Creativity and language

It is time now to return to the question of creativity, and to make concrete what is implied above. Non-human vertebrates all seem to possess comparable intellectual capacities; those capacities may be relatively simple, foremost amongst them being the capacity to form associations. And the use of those capacities in problem-solving clearly does not suggest any process of creativity in animals.

Something must, of course, be said about humans. It is clear that we can solve a virtually infinite range of problems which are insoluble by non-humans. We are, then, more intelligent than they, and the question which inevitably arises is, wherein lies the difference between our intelligence and non-human intelligence? Any answer to this question must be contentious and speculative. My inclination is to go along with those who argue that the basic difference lies in the human possession of language, and in its absence in animals. This view supposes that language learning involves more than association formation, that it requires devices, innate in humans, which are simply absent in non-humans. And it may not be too far-fetched to suggest that creativity is a fortuitous by-product of language. The possession and use of language may enable us to conceive of a problem in a virtually infinite number of different ways, and those humans who make the best use of this capacity for varying their conceptualisations may be the ones we lesser mortals call creative.

Acknowledgement

I thank Dorothy Hourston for her helpful discussion and criticism of the ideas contained in this paper.

Further reading

For a clear account of the origins of comparative psychology, including a discussion of Koehler's work, see:

R. A. Boakes (1984), *From Darwin to Behaviourism*, Cambridge: Cambridge University Press.

Detailed support for many of the claims made in support of the 'null hypothesis' may be found in:

Macphail, E. M. (1982), *Brain and Intelligence in Vertebrates*, Oxford: Clarendon Press.

The original reports of the two pigeon analogue experiments were as follows:

Epstein, R., Kirshnit, C. E., Lanza, R. P. and Rubin, L. C. (1984), ' "Insight" in the Pigeon: Antecedents and Determinants of an Intelligent Performance', *Nature*, **308**, pp. 61–2.
Boakes, R. A. and Gaertner, I. (1977), 'The Development of a Simple Form of Communication', *Quarterly Journal of Experimental Psychology*, **29**, pp. 561–75.

Index